# PRAISE FOR *CRACK THE CODE*

"Creativity is a skill. You can learn it, and you can get better at it. Here a
some of the key building blocks that you and your organization can use to st
solving the problems that matter."
**Seth Godin, Author, *The Practice***

"*Crack the Code* is the secret combination we've all been looking for to unl
innovation and creativity. This masterful work reveals surprising insights to k
boost creative capacity and open up a whole new perspective on business
life. Inspiring and actionable, the book delivers a roadmap to achieve be
results, conquer challenges, and seize potential."
**Josh Linkner, *New York Times* bestselling Author; Tech Entrepreneu**

"*Crack the Code* is a must-have survival manual for business leaders who
to build companies that last. Each chapter provides pragmatic applications
have immediate impact in a modern corporate environment."
**Drew Wolff, former CFO, International and Channel Development, Starl**

"Creativity has never been more important to business success as we al
to navigate and thrive in an environment of continual and seismic ch
Read *Crack the Code* NOW for practical, yet inspiring coaching on k
embrace and leverage creativity. A combination of rigorous, accessib
interesting thoughts, tactics, and examples that can help anyone unloc
own creative potential."
**Yin Woon Rani, CEO, MilkPep**

"Business leaders and companies find themselves 'locked' into how th
traditionally done things, unable to break free and break out. *Crack t*
provides what those who want to create innovative cultures need. Kais
you how to unlock creativity, embrace risk, and open up the potentia
people and businesses."
**Gary David, PhD, Professor of Sociology, Bentley Universit**

"*Crack the Code* is a highly effective playbook for injecting innovation into your organization. Kaiser delivers actionable advice, practical tools, and inspiring stories. If you want to unlock your creativity, this book is for you."
**Brian Krull, Global Director of Innovation, Magna Exteriors**

"*Crack the Code* is a must-read for anyone. It teaches you how to take complex problems and make them into opportunities. Kaiser's use of humor and gripping storytelling will leave you on the edge of your seat!"
**Nir Bashan, Clio Award–Winning Expert on creativity; Author,**
***The Creator Mindset***

# CRACK

## THE CODE

**www.amplifypublishing.com**

*Crack the Code: 8 Surprising Keys to Unlock Innovation*

**For more information, please contact:**
Amplify Publishing, an imprint of Mascot Books
620 Herndon Parkway #320
Herndon, VA 20170
info@amplifypublishing.com

Library of Congress Control Number: 2021907798

CPSIA Code: PRFRE0621A
ISBN-13: 978-1-64543-564-8

Printed in Canada

*To Jeff, Rene, and the entire Chin family, who so generously gave our family the gift of life.*

# CRACK THE CODE

## 8 SURPRISING KEYS TO UNLOCK INNOVATION

### KAISER YANG

COFOUNDER OF PLATYPUS LABS

amplify

# CONTENTS

## MINDSET 4

## CONNECTING IT ALL TOGETHER

## QUICK REFERENCE GUIDE

# INTRODUCTION

*We are living in unprecedented times.*

Believe it or not, I wrote the first line of this book in February of 2020. Now, in the late autumn of 2020, that sentence has become a ubiquitous mantra across the world. The coronavirus (COVID-19) pandemic has disrupted every life and taken many, pushed our health systems beyond their capacities, and created a global economic crisis that has affected every industry.

It has marked the end of both the longest period of positive job growth and the longest economic expansion in US history. It has decimated our industrial production and manufacturing and caused the steepest quarterly drop in economic output in recorded history. It has created simultaneous supply shocks, demand shocks, and financial shocks. Every worker, every leader, and every company has been impacted on a scale and at a speed that is truly, well, unprecedented.

And yet, my message hasn't changed.

Because, even before COVID-19, we were living in unprecedented times. Times of exponential complexity, dizzying speeds, disruptive technologies, shifting demographics and ideologies, geopolitical turmoil, and ruthless competition. The economic downturn has only made the truth obvious to everyone: the world is changing, becoming more complex and difficult, and the traditional models we rely on to lead, innovate, and grow must evolve to meet the challenges of today and tomorrow. We cannot cling to our past successes; we cannot rely on our previous models and expect to win. We must innovate.

Leaders across every industry were concerned about our failing traditional models far before the pandemic lockdowns threw our reality into sharp relief. In 2019, 55 percent of the participants in PwC's Twenty-Second Annual Global CEO Survey claimed, "We are not able to innovate effectively." The 2019 AON Global Risk Management Survey illustrated that five of the top ten risk factors on CEOs' minds directly tied to their organization's ability to harness innovation. In the 2020 C-Suite Challenge report published by the Conference Board, "building an innovative culture" was listed among the top three most pressing internal concerns of 740 CEOs surveyed globally. Even in the midst of the previously *unprecedented* economic heyday, leaders were increasingly aware of a trend my team at Platypus Labs named "the 70/30 rule": that relying on established processes, previous knowledge, and existing systems would only get you 70 percent of the way toward your potential. To crack the code, meet the challenges of the day, and enjoy sustainable success, you need to harness that final 30 percent.

# HOW?

We must defy traditions, seek fresh approaches, bounce back from missteps with more imagination, and invent and reinvent as we go. We must adapt in real time. We must place a premium on, we must challenge ourselves to, and we must exercise our abilities to *creatively solve problems.*

The greatest technology today is not machine learning, virtual reality, robotics, or even quantum computing. It is human creativity. We live in the age of creativity—yes, even now (especially now). Human creativity is the one true source of sustainable competitive advantage. It fuels all growth and progress and directly contributes to mission-based pursuits. Human creativity can't be outsourced or automated; in most organizations, it's one of the greatest untapped natural resources. It is prized above all other skills in the job market: LinkedIn analyzed over twenty million job posts to reveal that creativity is the number-one job skill employers have searched for on their platform for the last two years in a row. Each year, the World Economic Forum publishes a list of the top ten most important, most competitive job skills, taking into consideration changes in technology, work environments, industry disruption, and a host of other factors. In 2015, creativity ranked number ten. In their 2021 projections for 2025, it has jumped to number five. Interestingly, analytical thinking and innovation was number one, active learning and learning strategies came in at number two, complex problem-solving number three, and critical thinking number four—so, by mastering the techniques of the creative problem-solver, you're well equipped with the five most valuable job skills today.

Creative problem-solving is the key to the economic environment we live in. It can help in all areas of your business, from attracting and retaining the best and brightest talent to facing your competition and constricting margins. What the world is facing now has only increased the urgency to find creative solutions, to leverage the most effective tactics of creative problem-solving, and to crack the code for every business and individual. Developing your creative problem-solving skills has become mission critical.

## WHAT DOES IT MEAN TO CREATIVELY SOLVE PROBLEMS?

My team at Platypus Labs has studied dozens of definitions, but to me, there's a simple answer:

> **CREATIVE PROBLEM-SOLVING:** The act of solving complex problems in unique and unorthodox ways. Discovering fresh, unconventional approaches that replace prevailing wisdom.

Creative problem-solvers are change agents. They stick their finger in the eye of conventional wisdom. They defy the status quo. They break and then rebuild things. They imagine. They create. Creative problem-solvers share an insatiable curiosity, a willingness to experiment with unconventional approaches in order to conquer their challenges, a desire to forgo traditional thinking in favor of fresh possibilities. They have been the source of progress for generations. Martin Luther King Jr. applied creative problem-solving tactics to racial injustice and protesting, Galileo to the scientific norms of his day, and Charlie Parker to traditional harmonic structures to become the father of modern jazz. Zuckerberg toppled Murdoch by embracing creative problem-solving in the twenty-first century just as David defeated Goliath with the same tactics in biblical times.

In the seminal *Innovator's DNA* study, professors from Harvard Business School spent six years analyzing more than three thousand executives and five hundred innovative entrepreneurs, including such high-profile names as Amazon founder Jeff Bezos and Michael Dell, founder of Dell Computers. They concluded that there are five skills that separate the most accomplished, innovative creative problem-solvers from the rest:

1. **THEY ASSOCIATE,** creating links between seemingly unrelated items. They connect concepts, things, and people in new, imaginative ways. By finding common threads and looking for similarities, overlap, or combinations, they unlock new forms of creativity.

2. **THEY OBSERVE WHAT IS HAPPENING IN THE WORLD IN GREATER DETAIL,** imagining what could be different. They have a heightened level of awareness of the world around them.

3. **THEY EXPERIMENT AND DABBLE,** constantly looking to discover fresh, new approaches. They are unafraid of failure and continuously run a variety of experiments to validate their ideas until they land upon the right ones.

4. **THEY NETWORK,** finding diverse people whose ideas challenge their own thinking and expand their perspective, knowing that discussing challenges with people who have divergent viewpoints can spark incredible insight and solutions.

5. **THEY QUESTION *EVERYTHING*.** They all have insatiable curiosity, asking "why?" "what if?" and "why not?" Having a beginner's mindset is at the core of their ability to creatively problem-solve.

Having spent years studying, analyzing, and being a creative problem-solver, I've noticed a few additional characteristics that separate us from the traditionalists:

| TRADITIONALIST | CREATIVE PROBLEM-SOLVER |
|---|---|
| Top-down | Bottom-up |
| Monolithic | Democratic |
| Few giant bets | Many small experiments |
| Protects old ideas | Creates new ideas |
| Static | Constantly changing |
| Rules-centric | Ideas-centric |
| Slow, clunky, lethargic | Fast, agile, urgent |
| Resource-heavy | Scrappy |
| Avoids risk | Embraces risk |

There are also some common and shared philosophies I've identified as the foundation to innovation—beliefs that will serve as the underpinning for your own creative problem-solving, allowing you to build a culture of innovation in your own organization and your framework for creating change.

There are also a few key mindsets that the creative problem-solver avoids at all costs. Remember the movie *Se7en*? Brad Pitt and Morgan Freeman are tasked with cracking the code to find a serial killer whose murders each speak to one of the seven deadly sins—a list that, although created back in the sixth century, makes for a horrifying premise even today.

While the original seven deadly sins devour the human soul, there's a new set of seven that gum up our imagination and creativity. Unlocking innovation defines success in the twenty-first century, but before you can crack that code, it's essential that you clear this carnage!

1. **FEAR:** The granddaddy of all creativity killers! Our most brilliant creative sparks can be extinguished in an instant by the fear of looking foolish, embarrassment, or even by the fear of success.

2. **RIGIDITY:** Business leaders pride themselves in being "heads down," focused on immediate deliverables, yet that narrow worldview prevents us from sparking our creativity and imagination. Allowing yourself to be "heads up" will help you discover new possibilities for change and growth.

3. **PREMATURE EDITING:** Great ideas get killed in the blink of an eye when we inject our linear, analytical left brain into the creative process too early. Ideation sessions are geometrically more successful when you check your left brain at the door. Let all the creativity pour out, and invite the editor in after the fact.

4. **GROUP THINK:** Thousands of breakthrough ideas are suffocated each day by the destructive forces of group think. Don't let the fearmongers dice up your idea to the point where it loses potency. Have the guts to stand by your original ideas, even if they ruffle some feathers.

5. **OUTDATED TRADITIONS:** Blindly saluting the past is no way to craft a successful future. If you run across a system, process, or idea that has "always been done that way," you've likely just stumbled upon something desperately calling for reinvention.

6. **PLAYING IT SAFE:** Playing it safe has become the riskiest move of all. Don't let perceived safety lull you into inaction. In my twenty-five years in business, I've seen that we consistently overestimate the risk of trying something new but underestimate the risk of standing still.

7. **THE STATUS QUO:** In today's hypercompetitive market, compliance is dead. The big wins go to those who challenge conventional wisdom and defy the status quo, rather than succumb to it.

# WHAT IF I'M NOT CREATIVE?

I've seen it often in boardrooms and meeting spaces spanning the globe: I use the word *creative*, and some people start squirming in their chairs. The thought of being creative makes them uncomfortable. *Innovative? Sure. But creativity must be the responsibility of another group or person . . .*

Creative problem-solving doesn't require a fancy title or limitless resources. Creative problem-solving doesn't have anything to do with lab coats, computers, or even hoodies. Creative problem-solving is imminently accessible to all of us, no matter our age, race, rank, gender, education, background, or political views.

In fact, one of the most creative problem-solvers I know, Mick Ebeling (whom you'll get to know better later in this book), firmly believes that it is part of us, a primal human quality: "We are all creative problem-solvers; we, as a species, are innately born to problem-solve. Sometimes you don't have the right tool, so you have to invent a new way forward." This book puts these valuable tools into the right hands—your hands—to help you, your company, and your community move forward.

Even if you're not sold on your innate creativity, I have good news: that Harvard Innovator's DNA study concluded that 80 percent of an individual's creative capacity can be learned. That's right—it is a skill that we can all learn and develop and apply toward innovative outcomes. That's why it's important to continuously exercise your creative muscles and expand your creative capacity.

Here's one quick, simple exercise to get your creative muscles warmed up. It'll take you less than two minutes to complete, so why not put the book down and give it a try?

- Grab a pen and a piece of paper, and draw thirty blank circles on it of approximately the same size or use the worksheet on the next page. It doesn't have to be perfect—you just need thirty blank circles.

- Next, set a timer for forty-five seconds, and try to use as many of the blank circles as possible. Try to turn the circles into as many recognizable objects as possible, like a smiley face or a clock.

- Ready? Set? Go!

## 30-CIRCLES WORKSHEET

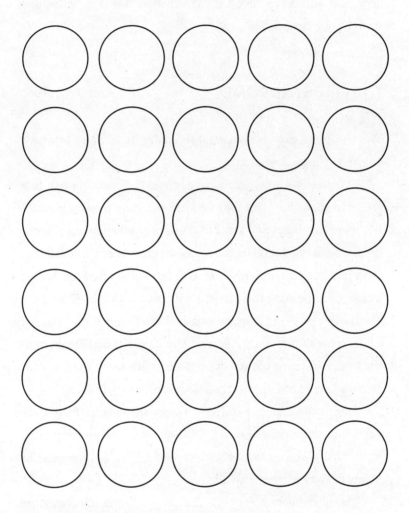

How many circles did you get? Ten? Fifteen? All thirty? Did you think about using two circles to make a pair of glasses or a bicycle? How about three circles for making a traffic light, or maybe a worm? Or multiple circles to make a polka-dot place mat or an LED light? The directions were intentionally vague to see if you would draw upon your internal creative skills' creativity to "break the rules" and stretch your imagination.

## THE PIKE SYNDROME

The 30-Circles exercise is a great reminder to be aware of what's known as the pike syndrome.

The pike is a fierce, cunning, aggressive freshwater fish that grows to about four feet long and can weigh up to sixty pounds. It's known to always find a way to get its prey, whether minnows or small waterfowl. Scientists conducted an experiment in which they put a pike in a tank with many smaller fish but blocked the feeding frenzy by separating the pike from its prey with a layer of glass. The hungry pike continuously smashed itself against the glass but couldn't break through the barrier. Eventually, it became discouraged and sank to the bottom of the tank. At that point, the scientists removed the barrier, giving the pike full access to its feast.

Except the pike continued to ignore the smaller fish—even when they swam right next to it. Unfortunately, the predator eventually died of starvation at the bottom of the tank, surrounded by plenty of tasty fish easily within reach.

This phenomenon, known as the pike syndrome, illustrates how we can become paralyzed by imaginary barriers. We may not even consider a whole set of possible solutions due to fear or some other nonexistent obstacle. Often the pike syndrome manifests itself in organizations when you hear comments like, "We've tried that idea before," or "Legal will never approve that approach." The pike syndrome also reminds us that we need to respond to changes in our environment. You may say to yourself, "My customers don't need that," or "My competitors will never do that," but we often succumb to the pike syndrome when we think we know too much about our business or our industry. At Platypus Labs, we like to use the 30-Circles exercise to illustrate that we need to challenge assumptions, to look beyond the obvious in order to explore new approaches and perspectives. It's an effective reminder that we must remove the imaginary constraints and boundaries if we want to solve our challenges and seize our opportunities.

Historically, we didn't need to fully develop our creative skills. With business cycles flowing over decades, the need to improvise wasn't important. We could discount the 70/30 rule and ignore the call to cultivate inventive thinking. But in the new era of disruption and change, we can no longer rely on the approaches of the past and expect the same results.

In the same way that interest compounds, your creativity gap will grow over time if not addressed. This has led to the downfall of many great organizations and will increasingly take a toll on both companies and careers. On the other hand, developing creative skills and mindsets will not only fill today's gap but also compound in your favor for years to come.

We must act with urgency to inject inventive thinking into our daily work. Your past training, experiences, systems, and approaches alone will keep you far from what's truly possible.

Even if your 70 percent is secure, it's time to discover your missing 30 percent.

Years ago, while conducting a workshop with a group of executives, I came across the most formal business executive in the universe: dark suit, pressed white shirt, conservative tie, and the general somber, serious demeanor of a television undertaker. I was responsible for unlocking his creativity, but I was getting nervous that I'd finally met my match.

When we started the RoleStorming exercise (which you'll learn in the chapters ahead), I cringed. There was no way he was going to loosen up for this. When he randomly drew his character card, I cringed again—Miss Piggy. Mr. Formal was supposed to live, laugh, think, and problem-solve as one of the lovable Muppets.

But, within moments, his jacket was off, his tie was undone, and he was throwing himself around the room like the dramatic diva pig. I had never seen a personal transformation like this before. Most importantly, the whiteboards were filled with crazy, new, innovative ideas.

I didn't teach Mr. Formal how to be creative; he had that inside him all along. We all do. It showed me that every barrier can be penetrated, even one as oversized as the role Mr. Formal played in his company and in his culture—a role that forbade such playful experimentation. I just had to trust in the exercises I've created to solve the problems they were designed to solve.

Applying creative problem-solving to business isn't a trendy hook I cooked up; it's a set of principles that I see in the world and actively use in my own life. Along with my team at Platypus Labs, I dedicate all of my time to helping businesses and individuals learn how to approach and solve their challenges and seize their opportunities more creatively.

Growing up in Tokyo among a business-minded family in an

international expatriate community, I've always been fascinated by how diversity of opinion and culture can help us learn, grow, and build creative collaborations. After graduating from the University of Michigan's business school program, I wanted to experience every possibility and build corporate experience across the spectrum, so I built a broad base of experience in sales, technology, operations, and marketing. I started out by working for large, global organizations such as Nortel Communications, Dole Foods Japan, and United Technologies, then spent the better part of the last twenty-some years helping to build successful technology start-ups, as well as starting a business of my own.

I've pitched global, large-scale digital and experiential campaigns to Fortune 100 clients, and I've also been behind the bar at the West End Grill trying to mutate a complete lack of experience to create the award-winning gourmet restaurant it is today. Throughout it all, the need to creatively solve problems—to find a way, to figure it out, to do it differently—has been the one commonality over the years. It's the ability to crack the code, to get things done, and to persist through adversity that have defined my career. My multidisciplinary approach to unlocking creativity and applying it toward productive, innovative outcomes has served me and every team I've been part of. That's why, in 2017, I knew I needed to share my insights and experiences with others: to help individuals and organizations drive growth and transformation by unlocking their own creative capacities. I cofounded Platypus Labs with other inspirational innovators who've found success in a myriad of fields through eerily similar creative problem-solving principles.

Through many rapid experiments, my secret weapon has been

the willingness to creatively solve problems, and it can be yours, as well. I've seen people crack the codes to their own seemingly insurmountable issues time and again using these strategies, and I've put our most inventive and helpful creative problem-solving tactics and mindsets in this book to inspire you and teach you to approach your own from a new angle. My goal is to help unlock your creative potential and systematically apply it toward the innovative outcomes that we are all searching for.

The creative problem-solving approaches in this book will become your most powerful system to meet expanding obstacles, challenges, and opportunities. They will help you crack the code, unleash your creativity, and find a way. The mindsets, tactics, and exercises can be applied to drive growth in any business setting, from a Fortune 500 biotech company to the corner dry cleaner, and at any stage in your career. They will teach you how to identify and overcome the barriers to creative problem-solving, apply proven tools and techniques to think differently and solve complex problems, strengthen critical-thinking skills to build your creative confidence, and infuse the creative problem-solver's mindset into your daily work.

Being a creative problem-solver is the new model for innovation, growth, and progress, and there is a systematic approach to harness this type of breakthrough thinking. This book is your tool kit, well organized and structured into four sections so you can refer back to your most-needed advice and exercises time and again.

Each section speaks to one of the four core mindsets common to all creative problem-solvers, followed by the two most powerful tactics to put the mindsets into action. Each tactic is defined and explained, followed by inspirational and illustrative examples of creative problem-solvers who have used it to tackle challenges of every shape and scope. After fully establishing the power and flexibility of the tactics when wielded purposefully, we'll delve into the targeted exercises you can use to strengthen your own abilities to bring your desired results to life.

- **MINDSET 1**: Every Barrier Can Be Penetrated instills self-confidence in your capacity to find a solution to any given challenge and to creatively problem-solve. It lays the foundation for your new solution system. This mindset is bolstered with the tactics of deconstruction (by which every barrier, no matter how tough, can be broken down, examined, and understood) and rapid experimentation (which provides a battering ram to efficiently break through the strongest defenses).

- **MINDSET 2**: Compasses Over Maps establishes the importance of exploring new paths to innovative solutions by changing where you start your problem-solving journey. This mindset is supported by the tactics of starting small (rather than waiting to find the map to your uncharted solution) and starting at the end (with the vision of the future your creative problem-solving will create).

- **MINDSET 3**: Nothing is Static thrills in living in a world that is constantly changing, recognizing that your ability to address challenges and create solutions requires you to constantly lean into what's next. This mindset is propelled into action with the tactics of the judo flip (leveraging oppositional thinking to reexamine the challenge) and the mash-up (forming alliances that create something entirely new).

- **MINDSET 4:** Diversity Is a Force Multiplier recognizes the importance of engaging with the world with people and ideas from beyond your silo, rather than isolating. With actionable tactics like imbizo groups (in which you engage with wide swaths of the community for meaningful exploration) and borrowed ideas (by which you train yourself to scan for the inspiration that surrounds you everywhere), this mindset opens up every possible solution in the world.

With this structure, we'll explore the eight critical tactics used by some of the best creative problem-solvers in the world and how they can be extracted and applied to help you navigate through ambiguity and discover new innovative solutions. You'll see real-world examples of how each tactic has been employed in a variety of business industries, communities, and products. These fresh approaches to creative problem-solving are designed to help you impact all facets of life—to grow your business, enhance your career, and help your community.

It's time to become the creative problem-solver you were always meant to be. The world needs the innovations you're capable of developing now more than ever.

Let's get started!

# EVERY BARRIER CAN BE PENETRATED

Successful creative problem-solving starts with this mindset alone: the inherent belief that no matter how difficult the challenge, there's *always* a way—that it *can* be solved by applying your creativity. You're ready to crack the code only if you believe that the code is crackable. Approach every problem, every step of a system, and every obstacle with the understanding that it can be overcome; the question is not *if* but *how*.

The most creative people in the world are no more superhuman than any of us. The key difference is that when they have a challenge or a setback, they don't throw up their arms and get discouraged; they are the ones who say, "Not yet," believing that every barrier can be penetrated (yes, even your biggest one—*especially* your biggest one!).

Assuming a problem can be solved is where your assumptions end—so enjoy and revel in the security of this fact. A core tenet of this first creative problem-solving mindset is a profound attraction to curiosity and exploration. Creative problem-solvers don't look at things as they are; instead, they constantly question every premise. Taking nothing for granted and assuming and taking nothing at face value, they ask an endless stream of questions about each problem they face and every element of prevailing wisdom. With the intensity of an inquisitive child, they refuse to accept life as it is, favoring instead what it *could* be and *will* be—once they crack the code.

## CLEARING MINES

There are over 110 million landmines planted beneath the Earth's surface, which kill and maim 20,000 people each year. The traditional approach to demining—more or less the same since the 1960s—is expensive, dangerous, and not all that effective. The UN estimates that for every 5,000 mines cleared, one clearing specialist is killed and two others are seriously injured. Though a landmine can be purchased for all of $3, professionally eliminating it hovers around $1,000. The cost to demine the world by the traditional method is estimated at $100 billion—an astronomical sum—and would kill 22,000 trained specialists and maim 44,000 more.

This worldwide issue is a terrifying daily threat to people in the desert regions of Afghanistan. Growing up just outside Kabul,

Massoud Hassani witnessed some terrible tragedies as a result of land mines, and as a young man, he made it his life's work to put at least a small dent in this giant problem. Massoud had no money, specialized training, or fancy credentials. He just refused to accept the notion that this barrier could not be penetrated.

Watching tumbleweeds blow gently across the desert sand inspired Massoud to create the Mine Kafon ("mine exploder" in his native language of Dari). The Kafon looks like a giant, ripe dandelion waiting to blow into the wind from its stem. The device is approximately six feet in diameter; it contains a central core, approximately fifty bamboo rods emanating from the center, and clay disks affixed to the end of each rod. The invention is light enough to be wind propelled like the tumbleweeds but heavy enough to detonate buried land mines.

In contrast to traditional approaches, the Mine Kafon is unmanned. This human toll is now eliminated. Further, the cost per land mine cleared has been dramatically reduced as the Kafon is over 120 times less expensive than classic methods. The Mine Kafon is the most important advancement in mine-clearing technology in the last eight decades, saving thousands of lives and millions of dollars. The design was so profound that it is now on permanent display at the Museum of Modern Art in New York City.

Massoud Hassani isn't ruminating in a celebratory glow. When my Platypus Labs team met him, Massoud was fully immersed in the next challenge: "Detonation is an important problem," he told us, "but detection is an even bigger issue. There are often miles of open space with only one landmine lurking to cause harm. After the success of the Mine Kafon in detonation, I've shifted my efforts to find a more comprehensive solution. I've reinvented it."

Today, Massoud is using low-flying drones to cover large swaths of land very quickly. He attaches a robotic arm with a high-powered magnet—a concept seen in practice on beaches across the world, where people use metal detectors to scan for lost goods. Once a mine is found, the drone places a Kafon on the site to eliminate it remotely and safely. In real time, Massoud's beaming back a video feed along with GPS coordinates so that newly detected landmines can be quickly located and conquered.

Massoud Hassani is a true master of this creative problem-solver mindset, and we can all learn from his example. When approaching any challenge, proceed as if everything is up for debate: no information is set in stone; no system is infallible; no solution is fixed. This mindset favors simplicity—sometimes the easiest, simplest solutions can be the most elegant.

## Beliefs

- Mountains exist to be scaled.

- It's necessary to break things in order to seek new outcomes.

- We assume nothing so we can beat everything.

- There's always a better way.

## Characteristics

- Disdainful of the status quo

- Disregards current systems

- Defiant

- Energetic and inspired by the possibilities

## Tactics

- Deconstruction

- Rapid experimentation

## TACTIC 1

# DECONSTRUCTION

In the classic heist movie *Ocean's Eleven*, the robbers extensively study the sophisticated and supposedly impenetrable security systems that protect their desired loot in order to find vulnerabilities. They order similar equipment and deconstruct it to see exactly how it operated so they could discover creative opportunities for infiltration. They practice each step, understanding the basic elements of each obstacle in order to perfect their plan of attack far in advance of their heist.

Though *Ocean's Eleven* is a fictional story, we see this level of deconstruction deployed every day to crack codes and solve problems. When a barrier seems impenetrable, creative problem-solvers immediately recognize that they must not be looking hard enough. Every challenge is complicated and has many moving parts—at least one of those moving parts is vulnerable. Cracking the code might well mean that you need to deconstruct the problem, whether your problem is a product, system, or company, to fully understand how it works and find that element most vulnerable to a solution.

As a creative problem-solving approach, deconstructing a system or process doesn't end with tearing it apart; as much as we can learn about a challenge by breaking it down, we have the capacity to discover even more by rebuilding it. When we put it back together, we can add, subtract, and substitute components to explore new possibilities and solutions. Deconstructing a beloved product down to its elements often results in innovations that open new markets, new revenue streams, and new utility. Think about it: subtracting caffeine from coffee created the multibillion-dollar decaf industry. Swapping a zipper for buttons enabled Levi's to produce millions of their popular button-fly jeans. Adding lump crab to the top of a steak in an elegant restaurant enhances both the meal and the restaurateur's bottom line. When facing an innovation challenge, creative problem-solvers often crack the code by examining their staples, isolating as many variable components as possible, and then experimenting with various additions, subtractions, and substitutions.

Deconstruction is powerful, especially when you think you're close—when you already have the tools, systems, or ideas that you need but they're not quite right or not performing at their best, starting with deconstruction allows you to honestly assess all of the pieces at your disposal. Then, working through possible solutions using addition, subtraction, and substitution, you can harness the raw potential of your original idea in a new, unimagined way.

## DECONSTRUCTION IN ACTION

Though deconstructing a product frequently leads to innovations we all recognize and enjoy each day, the scope of what a deconstructed "product" can be is wide ranging. These creative problem-solvers have eschewed tradition, traveled the world, and thoroughly dissected and reinvented the ways we think about everything from zapping bugs to riding a bike.

## LASER FOCUS

Pablos Holman is an expert at creatively solving problems, large and small. He's also a vocal proponent of spreading creative strategies to unlock innovation and believes that these keys can—and should—be taught.

Creative problem-solvers are in the business of breaking things. I don't think it's particularly weird or audacious. Creative problem-solving is just a learning style or methodology. Rather than relying on the instructions, we'll just try everything. We'll take something apart, break it into a lot of little pieces, and figure out what we can build from it.

For the last seventeen years, Holman has been a member of the Shmoo Group, a self-labeled "notorious group of creativity hackers." He loves doing live demos where he instantly accesses audience members' "secure" credit card info and computers, revealing passwords and other data. With a deep-seated belief that every barrier can be penetrated and the thorough use of deconstruction, he's the ultimate creative problem-solver.

Holman and his fellow barrier busters at Intellectual Ventures thoroughly attacked a barrier that many would consider impossible to eradicate and, through their deconstruction of the issue, stumbled across a highly implausible solution. Their target? Mosquitoes.

Now, mosquitoes aren't just a nuisance—they carry deadly viruses and diseases like malaria, which alone kills over six hundred thousand people per year. Bed nets, antimalarial drugs, and insecticides have helped, but according to the World Health Organization, malaria still ranks as the seventeenth-most-frequent cause of death, ahead of lung cancer, traffic accidents, and diabetes. Conducting a series of simulations to explore how malaria continues to spread throughout Africa, Holman and his team exposed new, unorthodox opportunities to stop the spread and ultimately eradicate this fatal disease.

They looked at chemicals, screens, and drugs, yet none of these yielded their desired breakthrough results; these solutions either weren't effective enough or harmed pollinators and other useful insects. They didn't want to slap mosquitoes on the wrist with half measures, and they didn't want to carpet-bomb the whole insect world. Deconstructing the process of effectively targeting an enemy, they decided to shoot down the mosquitoes with lasers.

The team devised a system to track the wing patterns of mosquitoes and then fire a deadly laser beam to take them out midflight. It is much like the Star Wars defense system but for mosquitoes instead of intergalactic nuclear missiles. The lasers can be mounted on posts around farms or in densely populated villages to create a photonic fence that eliminates the pests before they have the chance to spread disease. This advanced system can distinguish between mosquitoes and other insects, allowing helpful bees and butterflies to pass unharmed. It can even distinguish between male and female mosquitoes based on their wing beats, killing only the females, which are the ones that sting humans.

To bring their invention to life, Pablos and his team didn't use combat-grade carbon fiber or billion-dollar computing power. Instead, they took the deconstruction tactic into their search for raw materials, tearing apart ubiquitous consumer electronics, such as Blu-ray players and laptops, for the common parts they needed to crack this code.

## FROM BUREAUCRACY TO BEAUTY

Deconstructing mosquitoes is one thing, but creative problem-solvers are frequently faced with challenges we cannot shoot away. Imagine, for example, your least favorite places. Which type of business in the United States do you think delivers the *absolute worst* customer experience? From scouring dozens of customer shame surveys, runners-up include cable companies, discount airlines, mobile phone carriers, taxicab companies, and home repair experts. But the top of nearly every list is reserved for a special kind of agony: the good old Department of Motor Vehicles (DMV—or however your state chooses to label it—from the Motor Vehicle Administration to the Secretary of State, the names change, but the experiences reported are eerily similar!).

What a soul-crushing, exhausting, demoralizing experience it is—waiting endlessly in a cold, uncomfortable environment just to battle with a rude and apathetic associate, all too aware that the excursion will likely end in defeat, with you shuffling off to find yet another piece of arcane paperwork listed nowhere on the website in order to start the process anew.

That's how Chad Price felt, too—but he set out to make a change.

When the North Carolina Department of Motor Vehicles decided to privatize their service centers, Chad bid and won on the contract for Holly Springs, a suburb of Raleigh. No, Chad wasn't a sadist—he was committed to cracking the code, flipping the whole DMV experience upside down, and completely reimagining it.

The first step was to take the whole process apart. Chad visited

DMV branches throughout the state and observed and deconstructed the painful customer experience. He talked to citizens, elected officials, DMV workers, and paper-pushing bureaucrats. He studied the traffic flows, paperwork, and physical locations. He personally observed and documented each step of the customer process, looking for ways to disrupt it. He needed to understand all the moving pieces and how they were connected so he could remove the agony and add some delight.

"At every step of the way, the bureaucratic establishment told me all the reasons a transformation couldn't be done," said Chad. "They dismissed my idea that a DMV could be a terrific experience and that I could make money at the same time. First, I wanted to prove it could be done, because everyone told me it couldn't. But I also felt we could make a business out of it."

His detractors had a point. The private DMV earns fees per transaction, and the market is limited by geography, after all. This captive audience has no choice but to visit, and the population won't change if the DMV experience is terrific or lousy. What's the incentive for doing better?

Today, when you enter Chad's DMV in Holly Springs, North Carolina, there are delicious, fresh-baked gourmet cupcakes waiting for you on the counter. Those pair well with the fresh smoothies, cold-pressed juice, and dozens of exotic coffee flavors they offer. There are fresh-cut flowers, area rugs, and a lovely play area to entertain children while parents conduct their business. Warm color tones, friendly smiles, comfy seating, free Wi-Fi, helpful associates with welcoming smiles that treat you as if you were at a five-star hotel . . . wait, is this *really* a DMV?

The experience isn't only pleasant; it's also efficient. You can use a mobile app to check in before your arrival and later receive a text when your number is coming up. Walk-ins speed through the check-in process on an iPad and are alerted with updates during their wait. Locals love the place so much, they've been known to come in for coffee and cupcakes just to hang out and read a book, even if they have no pressing business at the DMV. Chad charges customers for the baked goods and beverages, which helps offset the added costs of the beautiful facility and highly paid, friendly workers.

Can you imagine a DMV ranked as one of the top facilities in the country for customer experience? Chad's is. But it gets better: "Since our service is so friendly and efficient, I have customers that drive up to one hundred miles to visit our location. They drive right past several other DMVs to get here, knowing that their round-trip time will still be less and they'll have a great experience too." That's right—after a thorough deconstruction, Chad refused to accept that his market size was fixed. He bet that a radically better experience would actually expand his customer base, and today, he's doing nearly twice the volume of any other DMV in the state. He's not only cracked the code and penetrated a heretofore impenetrable barrier; he's making top dollar and serving his community in a profoundly better way.

It's easy to feel stuck doing things the way they've always been done, but the Holly Springs DMV shows that the only real boundary is our own imagination. Take a nitty-gritty look at every detail of your most established notions and practices, and apply this same sense of creative wonder.

Regardless of the challenges you face, from internal process to external products, from HR policies to environmental impact initiatives, deconstruction is a potent key for unlocking innovation. Take apart existing structures, break them down to their core building blocks, and then tinker with alternatives to explore new possibilities.

## F*** THE UCI

What about challenges that involve a bureaucracy you can't take over? In most industries, there's a governing body that defines the rules of what can and can't be done; in bicycle racing, it's the Union Cycliste Internationale (UCI). Under their watch, there are strict limitations and rules that govern acceptable practices for bike design, and the UCI has the ultimate say as to which bikes will be allowed in competitive races such as the Tour de France.

Starting with a passion for bicycles, Robert Egger, creative director of Specialized, set out to upend the status quo: "I just believe, and dream, that bikes can be so much more . . . that there's no perfect design. The bicycle, although it's been around a long time, has much room for improvement. We can add so many great things . . . to make it much more than just a bicycle."

Robert wondered what he could design if he tossed the rulebook in the trash. The result? The FUCI Bike. (Yep, the name stands for "F*** the UCI.")

Robert and his team set out to completely shatter acceptable practices in order to reimagine what a bike could be and began by deconstructing their beloved product down to the individual components. They examined every aspect of the bike's design and construction, from materials used to the very basics of bicycle man- ufacturing. They deconstructed the UCI rule book, taking apart each regulation and challenging themselves to defy them. If a rule was printed, the team sought to break it.

To begin, the team looked at the most fundamental rule: that both wheels need to be the same size. In true creative problem-solver form, the team decided on a design in which the back wheel, at almost three feet in diameter, is significantly bigger than the front. This change leads to better performance in hilly conditions. The rule-balking FUCI has headlights and brake lights, added elements forbidden by the governing body that clearly enhance safety for nighttime riding. These lights, along with a small motor that gives riders an extra boost when needed, are powered by another forbid- den element: a lithium battery in the kickstand. Naturally, the bike has smartphone integration, which not only allows real-time data about rides and routes but doubles as a security feature, disabling the bike if the proper phone is not connected. The FUCI has a small trunk for storing valuables, small tools, or spare parts. According to the UCI, "Any device, added or blended into the structure which has the effect of decreasing resistance to air penetration such as a protective screen" is strictly forbidden. Egger and his team built a sleek windshield into the FUCI, which protects against flying bugs and road debris and increases the aerodynamic nature of the bike.

While the bike is strictly forbidden from competitive use, it is a hit among consumers and enthusiasts. Its commercial success illustrates the power of bold, defiant thinking in action. It demon- strates what's possible by deconstructing existing rules, challenging assumptions, and then rebuilding something fresh and new.

This type of heretical deconstruction is often considered the exclusive purview of the start-up—so would it surprise you to know that Specialized has been applying these types of creative problem-solving approaches since 1974? Mike Sinyard founded the company with a new take on bike tires, and the company has followed up with a string of disruptive innovations, including the Stumpjumper, the first major production mountain bike in the world, which is now displayed at the Smithsonian Institution in Washington, DC. Deconstruction and defiance make history.

## SARDINES TO THE RESCUE

Is there a more visible marker of defiance than graffiti? When you think about graffiti, you might imagine kids with criminal tendencies marking underpasses under the cover of night or urban artists, like Banksy, creatively reimagining their blighted landscapes. Whatever image you're conjuring up, it's probably not a fifty-two-year-old "tagging" old water tanks and trains with colorful paint for publicity.

Almost twenty years before Ed and Bonnie Seymour even invented spray paint, Robert Fergusson was painting colorful patterns on rusted equipment across Chicago. A creative problem-solver at heart and knowing that the whole world was looking at Chicago as it prepared for the 1933 World's Fair, Fergusson moved to the Windy City and embarked on a guerilla marketing campaign to drum up attention for his new paint.

Fergusson had spent most of his life at sea, from whaling boats in his youth to merchant marine vessels during World War I. He'd been fascinated with the coating used to cover ships' decks, a mix of fish oil and flake graphite that protected the steel from rust. Unfortunately, all that fish oil smelled awful and took ages to dry.

While working at a ship maintenance facility in New Orleans after the war, Fergusson began deconstructing the formula, systematically isolating each ingredient, and tinkering with alternatives. He traveled the world looking for just the right ingredients, visiting commercial fisheries from San Diego to Alaska. Only after countless experiments did he land on the keeper: processed oil from the pilchard sardine. Through deconstruction and isolation, he created a whole new formula that didn't smell like rotting fish carcasses and dried quickly.

Fergusson founded Rust-Oleum in 1921, which not only remains a household name but retains that spirit of deconstruction. The company has dozens of products and subbrands that were derived from deconstructing the formula and adding other ingredients, such as epoxies, latex, and alkyds. Today, Rust-Oleum has over one thousand employees and over $1 billion in annual revenue.

## WHISKEY WITHOUT LIMITS

Deconstruction is one of the easiest ways to dive into creative problem-solving for everyone because we all have a lot of experience with it. Every recipe is just the deconstructed individual elements—and we've all been in the kitchen and realized we might not have paprika, but red pepper flakes might fill the gap. Even if you've never touched a stove in your life, I know you're a master of culinary deconstruction—there you are, realizing the addition of ketchup with a little mayo will make those fries sing!

Of course, some people hold some recipes sacred; they're convinced there's only one right, true, and proper way to make apple pie, potato salad, lasagna, and what have you. And it's usually the way Grandma or some other esteemed elder did it. As an industry, that pretty much sums up big whiskey.

Cleveland Whiskey is a pretty new company, particularly for premium-priced bourbon, but they're already bringing home major awards. In an industry still more art than science, saturated in romance and old traditions, Tom Lix should fit right in. After all, he learned how to distill more than forty years ago in the navy, and his first experiments in spirits were more akin to bootlegging than laboratory environments.

But he'll be the first to tell you he's not running a craft or a microdistillery. In fact, he doesn't think of Cleveland Whiskey as a distillery as much as an innovative technology company—one of the most scientific and innovative whiskey labs in the world.

Recognizing that the majority of flavor in whiskey comes from the maturation process, Tom has deconstructed whiskey making to create finishes that simply have never been available before—without a single oak barrel in sight.

Instead of following the time-honored tradition of aging raw whiskey in charred wooden barrels for years or even decades, Tom tore apart the entire whiskey-making process and rebuilt it from scratch. He puts his raw whiskey in stainless-steel vats and throws chucks of charred wood in. Through a combination of pressurization and oxygen, Tom proudly makes his whiskey in a matter of weeks. Tom's process is not only faster—it creates new possibilities. Cleveland Whiskey's bourbons can be finished with transformative woods—black cherry, hickory, sugar maple, honey locus, and apple—that could never be made into barrels.

In his 1984 book *Hackers: Heroes of the Computer Revolution*, journalist Steven Levy wrote, "Hackers believe that essential lessons can be learned about the systems—about the world—from taking things apart, seeing how they work, and using this knowledge to create new and more interesting things." Creative problem-solvers—innovation hackers of every persuasion—can and should deconstruct their challenges, regardless of their shape and size. Deconstruction is a process of creative discovery, a methodology for innovation and growth, and a powerful engine of prosperity.

## DECONSTRUCTION: TRY IT OUT

Are you eager to deconstruct and crack the code of the challenge you're staring down? Try the SCAMPER technique!

Though my team and I did not invent SCAMPER (that honor goes to Bob Eberle), it is one of our favorite techniques to teach and one of the most popular for our clients who feel they are more logical and analytical than "creative." The structure of it forces us to deconstruct a challenge down to the roots and examine it from seven different sides, coming up with solid answers and a better understanding of it.

SCAMPER is an acronym for (S) substitute, (C) combine,

(A) adapt, (M) modify, (P) put to another use, (E) eliminate, and (R) reverse. You don't have to go in SCAMPER order (you can jump from adapt to reverse to substitute if that's what works best for your challenge); the most important part is that you hit them all.

Create a matrix that looks like this: SCAMPER categories in the left-hand column, and across the top row, list out specific elements of the product, services, or experience that you're trying to improve. Be as specific as possible, deconstructing it down to the smallest components. Once you've identified the elements of your product, service, or experience, randomly select the SCAMPER categories to apply:

- **SUBSTITUTE:** What parts of the product/service/solution can be replaced with an alternative? Examples of substitution could be replacing one ingredient with another, replacing a member of the team, swapping the release dates for a product, swapping retail locations—any change to any part of the equation is on the table for examination!

- **COMBINE:** What two parts of the process or product can be merged? Examples of combining could be completing two currently separate steps of manufacturing at the same time, combining two products or technologies into one package, and combining resources with a partner.

- **ADAPT:** What could be changed for better results? Examples of adapting could include adjusting the product or making the process more or less flexible.

- **MODIFY (MINIFY OR MAGNIFY)**: What about the overall process or how we look at this problem could be changed? Examples include considering whether your challenge would be alleviated by a massive shift in the number of consumers you have, market conditions, product size or shape, etc.

- **PUT TO ANOTHER USE**: How could you repurpose your current product or process? Examples include thinking about completely different market segments that could possibly use your product and examining whether the "waste" that you create in the manufacturing process could be used to create a different product.

- **ELIMINATE OR ELABORATE**: What parts of your current product or process can be completely removed? Examples include anything, big or small, that could be unnecessary or redundant.

- **REVERSE/REARRANGE**: What part of your process could be reversed or rearranged for better, more efficient, or more innovative production? Examples include looking at your assembly line or your go-to-market strategy.

There are a number of different ways you can utilize the SCAMPER technique, but this worksheet on the next page is how we like to do it.

- Across the top row, list out all of the features of the product, process, or experience that you're trying to innovate. In this sample worksheet, there are only a handful of columns, but use as many as you need.

- Randomly pick a SCAMPER category and start dropping in your ideas. We recommend a random approach in order to let your imagination flow, but you may want a more systematic approach. That's okay, you can customize it the way you want, but the goal is to apply as many of the SCAMPER categories to your challenge as possible.

# SAMPLE SCAMPER WORKSHEET

## PRODUCT, PROCESS, OR EXPERIENCE FEATURES

| | | | | | | | |
|---|---|---|---|---|---|---|---|
| | | | | | | | |
| Substitute | | | | | | | |
| Combine | | | | | | | |
| Adapt | | | | | | | |

|  |  |  |  |
|---|---|---|---|
|  |  |  |  |
|  |  |  |  |
|  |  |  |  |
|  |  |  |  |
|  |  |  |  |
| Modify or Magnify | Put to Other Use | Eliminate | Reverse or Rearrange |

# TACTIC 2

# RAPID EXPERIMENTATION

The art of creative problem-solving involves seeking to uncover the most elegant solution by trying numerous approaches to overcome an obstacle. Even if an approach delivers a positive result, the relentless pursuit of a better way drives the creative problem-solver to search for an even better approach.

Rapid experimentation is about using a battering ram (or three), not picking a lock. Trying lots of solutions to narrow down the best options quickly, which ultimately might lead to an elegant solution—or a messy one or somewhere in between. No matter what the solution looks like, you'll know it's the best one—because it works best on your problem. Too often we place the weight of the world on our shoulders, believing we must dream up a transformative innovation and then bet the company on its success. Creative problem-solvers take a more effective and less risky approach: instead of thinking of innovation as a single gigantic effort and getting overwhelmed by the task of inventing one groundbreaking thing, they dream up dozens of little ideas. In that way, rapid experimentation not only drives innovation—it reduces risk.

Rapidly cycling through experiments is a powerful strategy early in the problem-solving process and also later, when testing existing assumptions. Large quantities of ideas can ultimately drive higher quality than selecting the easy, obvious answers that emerge when selecting from a smaller pool of options. Rapid experiments can help you uncover small windows of opportunity, which can be expanded through other creative problem-solving approaches. It is also the right tool when raw persistence is needed, such as high-volume sales calls or hundreds of clinical trials for a new drug therapy. Your goal is to rapidly experiment to learn and get smarter, not just to work harder.

## RAPID EXPERIMENTATION IN ACTION

One of the most interesting elements of the rapid experimentation approach is that creative problem-solvers often don't use it to tackle a single challenge—they base their entire business models around it. The resulting constant stream of innovation is fun and addictive enough to build industry empires.

### BAGEL BASKETS

Back in 1999, Drew Greenblatt wasn't looking to experiment with anything; he just wanted a company that would produce stable, consistent income. He ended up buying Marlin Steel, a small manufacturer that made just one product: wire bagel baskets. Since it was such a small market, the company had few competitors; with just eighteen employees, Marlin Steel was able to drive consistent year-over-year revenue of $800,000 selling their specialty baskets to Einstein Bros., Bruegger's, and the hundreds of independent bagel shops throughout North America. What could possibly go wrong?

Well, within a few years, Chinese manufacturers started making and selling the same steel baskets at a price point 50 percent lower than Drew was charging—less than the cost of his raw materials. To make matters worse, anticarb diets shifted consumer demand for bagels from fad to forgotten. Sales were plummeting, and profits had evaporated into losses.

Marlin Steel was on the brink of collapse when Greenblatt's telephone rang. "It was an engineer from Boeing," Drew says. "He didn't think I was in the bagel basket business. He just needed custom wire baskets." He was in need of just twenty baskets to transport airplane parts throughout their factory. Unlike bagel baskets, which rarely required rush delivery or manufacturing exactness, this buyer needed precision baskets within one sixty-fourth of an inch of his specifications, and he needed them fast. "I told him, 'I'll have to charge you $24 a basket,'" Greenblatt said. "He said, 'Yeah, yeah, whatever. No problem. When are you going to ship them?'"

Drew didn't mind the precision or rush. What really captured his imagination was the buyer's total disregard for price. "I'm trying to sell a basket for $12, the bagel shops are saying, 'I'm not paying more than $6.' I'm ready to jump off a bridge, and here's a guy who just shrugs at the outrageous sum of $24. I was like, Wow. He's price insensitive." This insight led to a transformational pivot.

With no allegiance to the past, creative problem-solvers unceremoniously drop things that aren't working in favor of new approaches. Drew Greenblatt used the Boeing request as an opportunity to pursue an entirely new customer segment: manufacturers who needed specialty metal baskets. He dumped the bagel business and pivoted the company in a new direction, where he could compete, grow, and profit.

It wasn't an easy transition. His first shipments were a series of rapid experiments, cobbled together, crudely rigged to get out the door. While shifting from a single-item supplier to a custom basket maker was tough, it was worth it to pursue a much bigger market. At the time, there were only 3,100 bagel shops in the United States, but there were 333,000 factories. Greenblatt set out to reinvent every aspect of his business, from production standards to design to logistics. His baskets now needed to have mission-critical reliability to hold everything from microchips to turbine blades. He needed to retool his sales approach as well, now pursuing manufacturing giants such as Toyota, Caterpillar, Merck, and GE. By performing a series of rapid experiments in not only his production process but also his sales channels and pricing strategies, he could explore moving his company in a new direction without shutting his doors for months or years to construct an entirely new business.

Greenblatt's pivot paid off. Marlin Steel now has $10 million in revenue, and the team is gunning for $50 million within five years. They've invested $3.5 million in robotics to modernize manufacturing and have carved out a profitable niche in a competitive field. Had Drew Greenblatt only viewed his company as a bagel basket producer, he'd likely have lost it all.

Rapid experiments are frequently behind businesses that successfully pivot their focus—which happens more often than you may think. Running a number of experiments to explore their markets, their products, and their capabilities (and seeing great potential in their results) has been the turning point for some of the most well-known companies:

| COMPANY | PIVOT |
| --- | --- |
| Berkshire Hathaway | Textiles to investment conglomerate |
| IBM | Punch cards to computers to IT services |
| Pixar | Animation tools to animated films |
| Suzuki | Looms to vehicles |
| EMC | Furniture to enterprise data storage |
| Instagram | Check-in app to photo-sharing platform |
| Nokia | Paper mill to phones to network services |

These pivots are game-changing transformations; yours don't have to be as dramatic. When looking to spur innovation, don't ignore opportunities for micropivots: slight shifts in internal processes; fresh approaches to customer loyalty; divergent methods for recruiting. Innovative, creative problem-solvers use rapid experimentation to attack their own products, processes, and services in hunt of better solutions. When stuck in a particularly pesky challenge, rapid experiments will help you explore how you can pivot your way to new heights.

## AMAZON DASH

Internal rapid experiments on your employees, your methods, and your products can transform an industry, but how do you go about performing rapid experiments on your customers? How do you get inside the heads and homes of the people you're trying to reach and convince them to participate?

Imagine you are pressed for time, but after procrastinating for nearly a week, you're finally out of clean underwear. You throw your clothes into the washing machine, grab the bottle of detergent, turn it upside down, and . . . nothing. Frustration mounts as you realize that you'll need to make a special trip to the store for more detergent—you're out of other options.

This frustration is exactly what the folks at Amazon are on the lookout for.

What began as an online bookstore has expanded into the third most valuable company in the world, with 750,000 team members intently focused on rapidly experimenting to discover what's next. Jeff Bezos, now the wealthiest person in the world, views the company as a living organism whose purpose is to constantly evolve and adapt to changing circumstances. Right from the start, he worked to build a company that was fluid in its offerings and approach. The only immovable principles have been an obsession with serving customers better and a commitment to ongoing innovation—to cracking the codes wherever they find them.

So how does this help you, standing in front of your washer without detergent or clean underwear? Instead of whipping the empty jug across the room in defeat, you press the small button affixed to the front of your washing machine. The button connects to your home Wi-Fi network, logs into your Amazon account, looks up your last order of detergent to ensure you get your favorite brand, and immediately ships you a fresh bottle, billing the purchase to your credit card. All with the single touch of an Amazon Dash button.

This little invention is one of hundreds that keeps Amazon on the forefront of change and progress. As you may expect, you can get a Dash button for just about anything. A Glad button inside a kitchen drawer can reorder plastic sandwich bags. Low on shaving cream? Press the Gillette button you placed in your bathroom. Paper towels, bug killer, dish soap, and even condoms are available with the touch of a button. Amazon is making it dead simple to do business with them.

Bezos has said, "A company shouldn't get addicted to being shiny, because shiny doesn't last." What dazzles a customer today will soon be commonplace, so he pushes his team to reinvent early and often. Through rapid experiments, Amazon has extended their reach from textbooks to space travel; with the Amazon Dash button, they're extending their reach into *Jetsons*' territory, and we're all helping run the experiment with them. Most recently, the team at Amazon released the Dash Smart Shelf, which automatically detects when supplies are needed.

## FASHIONABLE FEEDBACK

Eighty-four-year-old Amancio Ortega doesn't necessarily look like the poster child you'd expect from the fashion industry; prior to 1999, no photographs of him had ever been published, and he refuses to even wear a tie. Certainly nothing in his early bio hints at the impact he'd have on the way the world dresses; growing up as the youngest of four children in a small town in Spain, he dropped out of school at the age of fourteen to pursue manual labor, like his father. Yet with no particular design expertise, resources, or education in the field, Ortega has amassed a net worth of over $70 billion as the founder of Zara, the world's largest apparel retailer.

Core to Ortega's success is how he's based his business off the principle of rapid experimentation. In the conventional fashion retail model, clothing designers dream up a new idea that they hope will be widely accepted. Perhaps they validate it with a focus group, but before long, the design is set. Next, millions of garments are produced in low-cost countries and shipped to retail stores for sale. Sometimes the design is a hit, but more often, a large percentage of inventory sits on the shelves for months. The brand spends millions in advertising to create demand, but eventually, as much as 35 percent of the goods are sent to discount stores to be sold for pennies on the dollar.

Zara takes a completely different approach. Ortega developed a method he calls "instant fashion," pioneering the design, manufacturing, and distribution processes to dramatically speed up time to market. This allows him to respond to new trends quickly and use rapid experimentation to topple competitors.

From their own centralized factories, Zara can design and ship a new product in less than a week. A new product idea starts with a micro production run; for example, when they design a new red dress, they may only produce and ship out 4,500 in that first week—two for each of the company's 2,250 stores. Rather than placing a big bet on an unproved design, the company relies on rapid experimentation and lets data drive their decisions.

Zara's highly sophisticated feedback system allows store managers to instantly report feedback on new products. Customers may say they like the dress, but the shade of red is too bright, or that they'd love it in a different length, or that it needs a zipper; this feedback is evaluated back at headquarters, and adjustments are made in a matter of hours. The next week, after implementing the design changes, 4,500 improved red dresses ship to the network of stores for another round of experimentation and feedback. Only after customer demand has been validated is the dress mass-produced.

Where most clothing manufacturers produce only a few dozen new styles each year, Zara launches over twelve thousand new items annually. Through rapid experimentation and continuous trial and error, Zara is able to keep inventory levels low and price points high. While competitors turn inventory only a couple of times a year, Zara is able to enjoy fourteen times the throughput. And while competitive brands frequently end up at the discount shops, you'll never see a Zara sweater at TJ Maxx. Through rapid experimentation and a continuous improvement loop, they eliminate that waste by adapting quickly to shifts in consumer taste.

## THE NETFLIX OF FITNESS

After earning his master's degree in computer engineering from the Georgia Institute of Technology, Yony Feng quickly moved to the heart of Silicon Valley. Courted by the top technology powerhouses for his masterful computer skills, Yony served in senior positions for both Cisco and Skype and earned his reputation as a top-notch engineer—curious, articulate, and whip smart, with the insightful wisdom of a Zen monk.

So how did he end up in New York at a fitness bike company?

Calling Peloton a fitness company is kind of like calling Apple a phone company: part stationary bike manufacturer, part content producer, and part tech company, Peloton is creatively problem-solving home fitness. With Yony leading the charge as chief technology officer, they have become the "Netflix of fitness," delighting customers, building a rocking company, and making society healthier.

From the Kickstarter-based launched in 2013, Yony and his team set out to replicate the energizing experience of a live class at the übertrendy SoulCycle or Flywheel Sports from the comfort and convenience of your own home. Peloton now offers both premium stationary bikes and treadmills with gorgeous built-in screens connected to the cloud, allowing home users to participate in dozens of live classes each day. Riders, runners, and yogis sweat along with the instructors in real time while seeing how they stack up to their classmates on an interactive leaderboard. If you don't see a live class that fits your needs, you can choose from over ten thousand prerecorded ones. The high-definition content streams to your screen, while your equipment updates itself automatically. Adjustments such as level, tension, and resistance change as you use it, all controlled by the software.

Peloton's 3.1 million customers are known for their cultlike fervor for the machines. "I get an incredible experience, just like at class," one gushed, "but it costs less, saves me time, and I get to do my workouts on my own terms." This loyalty is echoed in the company's growth, with revenues increasing from $0.4 billion in 2018 to $0.9 billion in 2019, marking an increase of 110 percent. The model became exponentially more attractive as the COVID-19 pandemic shut down spin studios and gyms across the world, and Peloton reported 218 percent growth year over year in the first fiscal quarter for 2020, even with all their bikes sold out. They are the breakaway leader in a whole new category of home fitness and content delivery.

Global events aside, Peloton's remarkable success can be traced back to their Kickstarter origins; their products are based on high-volume, rapid experimentation, specifically developed to make customers fall in love.

"We conduct tons of experiments to improve the riding experience," Yony explains. "We carefully study how our suite of products, technology, and content make our customers feel. In order to have riders truly feel like they are in class, we are constantly fine-tuning the experience. We test dozens of seating options, handlebar styles, and pedal choices. We test sound, lighting, and music. We bring in riders to our New York studio and experiment with tiny fluctuations, such as the angle of the screen, to improve the overall experience."

Rather than the traditional new product approach, launch big and launch final, Yony lives in an ongoing state of creative problem -solver flux. A massive number of experiments, testing and controlling even the smallest details and then refining along the way, has been the underpinning of Peloton's success.

Continuous rapid experimentation can be used to improve all aspects of our business lives, from product to process to leadership. A series of expandable yet controlled experiments is a far more effective approach to the nail-biting fear of universal change. Run an experiment with a new interview process for hiring fresh talent. Try out a new customer service experiment and see what the results show. Test how a new cold-call script measures up against the status quo in a quick, three-day experiment in one market. If the data is encouraging, expand the test. If not, discard the idea and try something else. Running a high volume of controlled experiments is your best chance at driving growth while mitigating risk. Test; measure; refine. Rinse and repeat. In the words of author and painter Hermann Hesse, "In order to achieve what is possible, you have to try the impossible over and over again."

## HOW TO RUN AN EXPERIMENT

The primary goal of rapid experiments is to make faster, more informed decisions. By quickly gaining evidence-based data from your stakeholders, you will

- dramatically reduce risk;

- minimize resources required;

- increase the number of ideas pursued; and

- end false positives and negatives.

Rapid experiments are all about learning and validation. Through experiments, you change opinions into facts, challenge your assumptions, and use data to validate your idea. You'll also discover surprises about your customer along the way. Don't get stuck in a long, drawn-out process that involves internal politics and compromise. Be fast and scrappy, and quickly find out if your idea will work.

- **STEP 1:** Create an opportunity statement that clearly defines your idea, a bold vision that answers these three questions:

  1. Who is your target customer?
  2. What is their main problem or pain point?
  3. What is your solution?

- **STEP 2:** Identify your key assumptions, the most important behaviors that *must* be true for your idea to work. You assume them to be true but have not yet proved it with evidence.

- **STEP 3:** Build your experiment. Develop the absolute minimum product or service offering required to test your assumptions. Your experiment doesn't have to be complicated. The goal is to remove enough uncertainty to move the idea forward. A simple brochure or video explaining your idea to your target audience can be highly effective. Document your hypothesis and minimum success criteria, and be sure you're measuring real customer behavior.

- **STEP 4:** Learn and decide. Review metrics from your experiment, and note any surprises you came across. Discuss why your hypothesis passed or failed, as well as any new customer insights you discovered. Decide if you will change your idea (pivot), continue on, or run additional experiments.

## Pro Tips

- Record exactly what happens, in detail. Videotape the experiment, if possible.

- Have an open mind. Be neutral and avoid confirmation bias.

- Embrace a beginner's mindset. Try to learn both why and why not. Savor the surprises and unexpected feedback.

If you need any help running experiments, reach out to us at innovate@platypuslabs.com!

## AMPLIFYING KNOWLEDGE

The best creative problem-solvers invest the time and energy to sharpen their skills. Within the mindset that every barrier is penetrable, both rapid experimentation and deconstruction rely on a creative commitment to learning in order to discover new, innovative approaches. To a large degree, a creative problem-solver's success is determined by how quickly they learn and iterate.

Einstein's famous theory of relativity ($E = mc^2$) is now just over one hundred years old; this elegant formula helps us understand how the world works. The business world has its own formulas for success: Hard work + Dedication = Results; Power = Money + Influence; Big > Small; Fast > Slow; Fancy Degree + Time = Corner Office.

The thing is, the world has changed. The old rules no longer carry the day as we cope with neck-and-neck competition, mind-numbing speed, and exponential complexity. Add in macro trends such as global markets, digitization, cloud computing, millennial workforce shifts, mobile technology, and geopolitical turmoil, and you're wrestling a whole new beast—one that can't be conquered or even accounted for with these long-expired formulas.

Creative problem-solvers use an entirely different formula for success:

**PROGRESS** = SPEED x LEARNING ÷ COST

In other words, the success of your business or career or even creative problem-solving will not be based on what you already know but on how fast and inexpensively you learn. While cash may have been the fuel of growth in the past, learning is the new energy supply. Fortunately, it's renewable, environmentally friendly, produces no waste, and is extremely low priced. Deconstructing your challenges will quickly show you what you need to learn; rapid experimentation will help you learn it in record time.

When calculating cost, the investment in learning (books, conferences, training, etc.) is like a rounding error compared to the real costs of not learning fast enough: opportunities squandered, time wasted, employee turnover, competitive losses, customer attrition, and damaged morale. To keep the true cost of learning low, learn as fast as possible. If you're not actively prioritizing learning, you may be unknowingly falling behind. Near-term competitive advantages come and go, but the learning organization wins in the long run.

Increasing learning speed goes back to the rapid experimentation approach. True innovators don't waste time overanalyzing which scheme may crack the code; instead, they deconstruct their challenge and throw high quantities of solutions at it all at once or in rapid succession, measuring which works the best. If you commit to read for an hour every day, you'll likely discover more answers than trying to select one perfect book for the year. When refining your craft becomes a daily habit, mastery ensues.

Push yourself and your team to learn more and learn fast, and your ability to innovate will skyrocket. Set learning objectives in the same way you set performance targets. Recap and share lessons learned. Experiment; measure; refine; learn.

## RAPID EXPERIMENTATION: TRY IT OUT

Ready to take your own challenges into the lab? You've already got solid instructions for how to run an experiment—here are some great methods and questions to ask yourself to really harness the creative potential of your rapid experiment:

1. Think of a key challenge you're facing in any aspect of your business. If you had to attack the problem with one hundred rapid experiments, what would the first five be?

2. List three areas of your business that feel stuck. Brainstorm at least ten ideas for how you could pivot each to uncover new possibilities.

3. What are three ways you could increase the force and velocity of your internal systems to amplify results?

4. What is your current corporate learning strategy, and how could making rapid experimentation a core portion of your culture up your game to a whole new level?

5. Layering the element of time into your creative process, what new ideas can you uncover with the following isolated time frames:

   A. What short windows of time could foster a successful new launch (seasonal, around a particular calendar event, etc.)?

   B. If your new idea could only exist for a limited time, what might you consider (limited-time product offerings, sales promotions, internal bonus periods, hiring initiatives, etc.)?

C. If you're facing a longer-term challenge or opportunity, how could you break it down into focused agile bursts to foster a more creative (and ultimately productive) process?

6. Organize a single-day hackathon. At first, take on a small or midlevel problem to generate momentum and post early results. (Later, once you're engaging in regular hackathons, you can tackle the big stuff.) If you need any guidance or you'd like to share a tip from your own hackathon, please reach out to us at innovate@platypuslabs.com; we're here to help!

# COMPASSES OVER MAPS

The leaders at software giant Intuit have a saying that all creative problem-solvers adopt: "Fall in love with the problem, not the solution." We are drawn to problems over solutions.

Cracking the code is the objective—not employing any one pre-ordained tool to do it. Every successful creative problem-solver is buoyed by curiosity and exploration; rather than desperately seeking a detailed master strategy to mindlessly execute, innovators journey down unmarked trails with creative confidence. Creative problem-solvers have a lot in common with history's great explorers —we have a general idea of where we're headed and what we hope to find, but we're armed with compasses, not maps.

Hold up, you may say—a map is a pretty handy tool. Who chooses a compass over an accurate map and a clear destination—

better yet, who even chooses a map anymore over GPS guidance? Plug and play—no thinking required. When the system tells you exactly how to navigate every twist and turn, you can focus elsewhere and simply comply. With self-driving technology developing at a rapid pace, we're coming up on a time when we won't even have to interact with those twists and turns—the GPS will be able to talk to the car and leave us out of it. That, you may argue, is innovation. That is progress.

That is cool, yes—but, as Doc counseled us in *Back to the Future*, "Where we're going, we don't need roads."

## NO BOSSES?

Valve, LLC, the company behind video game hits such as *Half-Life*, *Counter-Strike*, and *Day of Defeat*, is valued at over $2.5 billion. We can easily conjure up images of the prototypical progressive company—people with funky titles, a foosball table in the break room, and a juice bar lurking somewhere—but Valve takes progressive to a whole new level. The company is the living embodiment of the compasses-over-maps mindset.

Gabe Newell is technically the president, but he has no direct reports. In fact, no one works for anyone at Valve. There are no bosses, managers, leaders, or even titles—everyone's job is simply to contribute as much value as possible. Much of their nontraditional, creative problem-solver philosophy becomes clear when reading their employee handbook: "A fearless adventure into knowing what to do when no one's telling you what to do."

Gabe founded Valve in the Seattle area in 1996, setting out to make great games and an even greater team environment. Coming from Microsoft's rigid policies and complex hierarchies, Gabe was determined to use a radically different approach. He wanted to create a culture that fostered greatness, creativity, and impact by removing any and all structures that could hamper innovation.

"When you're an entertainment company that's spent the last decade going out of its way to recruit the most intelligent, innovative, and talented people on Earth, telling them to sit at a desk and do what they're told obliterates 99 percent of their value," Gabe declared. So he created "flatland," a completely flat organizational structure.

Team members pick their own projects to work on without a single directive. They choose to spend their completely unstructured time in whatever way they believe will create the most value. All teams and projects are temporary, as are all desks. Each workstation is on wheels, allowing teams to be formed, grown, or disbanded with ease.

Valve is a company without maps. There are no schedules, orders, or preset processes. If you want advice, ask a colleague. If you need help, lean over and ask your peers. People at Valve are very vocal, since they have a strong sense of ownership, but no one has to listen to anyone else. Decision-making is completely decentralized, with the core belief that the wisdom of all is better than the judgment of one.

Traditional managers may be horrified and quickly dismiss the lack of structure as far too risky. However, Valve isn't a disorganized mess; productivity is sky-high compared to others in the sector, and, armed with just a compass pointed at producing the best games possible, they are growing at a dizzying pace, with record profits.

Using a map is perfunctory; it presupposes both the destination and the best way of getting there. But with today's furious speed and mind-numbing complexities, there's no such thing as a map to success. Business victories now involve pioneering new ground, requiring the equivalent of off-roading through uncharted territory. Creative problem-solvers gleefully grab a compass and interact with the realities of the landscape, adjusting course based on the lay of the land instead of carefully retracing the mapped-out routes of previous solutions. This mindset sees a mountain as an opportunity, not an obstacle. We draw up the maps so others can follow. We figure it out and find a way and live to do it.

## Beliefs

- We fall in love with the problem, not the solution.

- It's okay to embark with no dedicated route.

- We embrace the thrill of the challenge.

- Microinnovations allow us to adapt quickly to changing conditions.

## Characteristics

- Extremely curious

- Adventurous

- Playful

- Courageous

## Tactics

- Start small

- Start at the end

## TACTIC 3

# START SMALL

How do you climb a mountain?

One step at a time.

Too often we can become paralyzed by the size and scale of the problem we are trying to solve. Too often innovation efforts are conceived of as the corporate equivalent of a military shock-and-awe assault. Rather than look at a challenge in its entirety, this tactic is all about finding a small win that allows you to begin making progress, then exploiting it to drive toward your desired outcomes.

The creative problem-solver mindset of compasses over maps fosters curiosity and exploration. It has us constantly on the prowl for little openings, the next foothold in the face of the cliff. They prefer dozens or hundreds of small beginnings to massive and risky bets and only double down when they've been successful in one of these endeavors. As you seek to tackle your own innovation challenges in any aspect of your business, start small, find your opening, and then fully leverage it!

A small, previously undetected opening that initially appears innocuous can ultimately lead to profound results. For example, if you are a salesperson selling office supplies to corporations, winning a Fortune 500 account is the ultimate accomplishment. Rather than trying to capture the entire company's business all at once, you may start by selling one small order to one small department. Then you can grow your business to other departments from inside the fortress walls. Sales professionals call this a "land and expand" strategy, which is the exact approach a creative problem-solver embraces when starting small.

When you're trying to grow your business and accelerate your career, starting small can be a powerful way to achieve your goals.

## STARTING SMALL IN ACTION

Starting small means that you can start anywhere; if you're in uncharted territory, this is a great way to create a massive impact. From setting new rules to creating business empires to discovering niche markets, I've chosen these examples of very small starts to showcase the sheer variety of ways that creative problem-solvers have changed the world using this approach.

## CHANGING THE CONSTRAINTS

In the early 1960s, Bennett Cerf, an editor at Random House Publishing, made a bet with a young children's author. The author's last book had been very simple and extremely successful—but he had used a whopping 225 words. Cerf was positive that he couldn't write a book using just 50 words of the English language.

Not one to back down from a challenge, the author sat down and started scripting his next story. After rearranging exactly fifty words dozens of different ways, the book was done, the editor had lost the bet, and a legend was born. With *a, am, and, anywhere, are, be, boat, box, car, could, dark, do, eat, eggs, fox, goat, good, green, ham, here, house, I, if, in, let, like, may, me, mouse, not, on, or, rain, Sam, say, see, so, thank, that, the, them, there, they, train, tree, try, will, with, would,* and *you,* Dr. Seuss launched from the success of *The Cat in the Hat* to *Green Eggs and Ham.* This exercise in starting—and finishing—small sold over two hundred million copies and helped him become one of the most important children's authors in history; the book is beloved by children all over the world to this very day.

Innovation and creativity have the power to disrupt businesses and change the world—and it can all seem like too much to tackle. When the need to change, innovate, and do things differently feels too big, it can be paralyzing. The key to unlocking the potential can be to start small—no, even smaller than that. Changing the constraints you have control over and making them even more constrictive is an excellent way to start small and liberate your creativity. It's a twist on dominant thinking; after all, who doesn't want to use every tool at their disposal? Well, if you're committed to not approaching things the way you always have, to forging new paths—then, you!

One of the most effective and popular constraints to self-impose has become time—tight deadlines are an excellent way to start small and get big results. "I don't need time. What I need is a deadline," legendary innovator, jazz composer, and bandleader Duke Ellington famously said. Adam Savage, industrial and special effects designer of *MythBusters* fame, agrees: "Deadlines refine the mind. They remove variables like exotic materials and processes that take too long. The closer the deadline, the more likely you'll start thinking waaay outside the box."

Hackathons (often called agile bursts) are a way to start small while combining the clarity of the extreme deadline with the creativity of rapid experimentation. Creative problem-solvers who don't have the time to pursue a patient approach instead hyperfocus on their efforts and sprint to their desired outcome.

The premise is to attack the challenge or opportunity with short bursts of dedicated activity, eliminating all other distractions. These can be one-week sprints, forty-eight-hour intensive sessions, or even two-hour bursts: a fixed amount of time coupled with extreme focus and intensity. Hackathons are all about speed—attack a problem hard, intensely, even completely, in a short span of time. Set a short deadline, and commit 100 percent of your attention.

The term *agile burst* came to prominence in 2001 with the publication of *The Manifesto for Agile Software Development*, drafted by seventeen software developers trying to elevate their craft. A core, revolutionary element was the notion of working in short sprints. Prior to the agile movement, a group of developers would all work on a large project for months, building up to a single launch date. In the new model, short sprints were established, followed by numerous smaller launches. Utilizing ranges from forty-eight hours to two weeks, developers worked fast to ship code to be tested, evaluated, and adapted many times along the way to a final launch.

Software engineers found that short, focused bursts under a ticking clock delivered more creative output and fostered better overall quality, as they could course correct early and often, and integrate rapid experiments into their workflow. The bursts also helped recalibrate resource needs along the way, delivering a more efficient project in the end. Having to quickly ship working lines of code forced the developers to get scrappy and find creative workarounds to obstacles and challenges. The parameters of the agile burst force the negativity out of the room, shifting the thinking from what can't be done to what can—what must be. Concerns around long-term execution, regulatory burdens, and corporate bureaucracy vanish, replaced by imagination and creative verve.

With a fixed, short window of time, teams are focused on a desired outcome, then throw everything they have at it in a flat-out sprint. Hackathons have been used to invent new companies, cure diseases, reimagine organizational structures, and craft new solutions for customer engagement. Some hackathons are internal, focusing on specific or company-based problems, while others are independently hosted gatherings to create new ideas, companies, and products from scratch.

Changing the constraints is a small start that can deliver big results!

## SORRY SEEMS TO BE THE HARDEST WORD

There are few words as simple and powerful as "I'm sorry." But when was the last time you got a genuine apology from a company that delivered a poor experience?

Martin McGloin is the CEO and cofounder of Sorry as a Service (SaaS), a company that helps some of Europe's biggest organizations start with the small, simple idea of apologizing and making it memorable and authentic.

Inspired by Mr. Larsen, a bank manager from his childhood who understood the old-school model of customer service, and a conflict with his mobile provider, Martin came up with an idea to help companies address customer churn—not by bringing in new customers but by repairing damaged relationships with their existing ones. Basically, he helps companies learn how to say they're sorry.

Reaching new customers has always been a challenge; with traditional and social media advertising, it can range from expensive to impossible. McGloin learned that for many companies, the best (and most cost-effective) way to bring in customers is to delight their existing customers. Happy customers tell their friends and families, geometrically building your customer base.

But if it's so simple, why are so many companies failing miserably? They're focusing on the wrong aspect of the customer experience. Companies train their reps to respond to complaints rationally, not emotionally; but for the customer, their bad experience *is* emotional, not rational. SaaS provides "an opportunity to empower customer service agents to not think about a complaint as something that needs to be rationally responded to, but instead think, how do you build an emotional relationship?"

SaaS started with a small, low-budget rapid experiment to test different apology options. They gave dice to customer service reps; when dealing with complaints, the reps would roll the dice. If they rolled 6, they'd give the customer a gift card; if they rolled 2, they'd send a hand-piped, personalized chocolate plaque. Every outcome had the same dollar value, and the results were staggering: a 35 percent increase in customer retention and an increase in their customer lifetime value, totaling an ROI over three times the initial cost of the apology.

One major SaaS partner in the UK who'd failed to deliver to a client in Germany sent a handwritten note and chocolates in apology. She replied in kind with a handwritten note of her own:

I had a bad experience when my transaction took a long time. Then I got a great chocolate from David, and I was pleased. It made me laugh. However, my husband now thinks that I have a lover in Great Britain. He can't believe that somebody from your company would send me a chocolate to say sorry. So creative a way to apologize.

This customer ended up sharing a laugh with the company that had let her down, and they'd so differentiated themselves with this small start that it was easier for her husband to believe she had a secret lover in another part of the world than that a company would send such an effective apology.

So how can a company learn to say sorry in unique, personalized ways and at scale? Sorry as a Service cheekily provides Software as a Service (the more well-known SaaS)—the model that has worked for big companies like Salesforce.com, Box, NetSuite, and Adobe. Your monthly fee buys cloud-based access to the Sorry as a Service software, updates, and support, which integrates into major CRM systems and custom platforms. They allow customer service reps to send out personalized sorries from hundreds of possibilities, including flowers, cookies, and chocolate, from right within their existing workflows. SaaS works with local sorry providers to make sure that the sorries are unique, personalized, and meet quality expectations.

From starting small with the simple apology, SaaS has delivered sorries to their users' customers in every country in the European Union. They're partnered with some of the biggest names on the continent, and their client list expands daily.

## THE SWEET SOUNDS OF INNOVATION

As a graduate student at MIT in the late 1950s, Amar was light on cash, but, scrimping and saving, the audiophile was finally able to purchase a top-of-the-line stereo system. But after months of sacrifice, he was deeply disappointed. What he'd hoped would sound like a concert hall more closely resembled a loudspeaker in a subway station.

The prevailing wisdom at the time was that sound quality was a function of power and speaker size; as he now had both at his disposal and *still* wasn't able to enjoy high-quality tunes with his friends, Amar wasn't convinced. Studying both audio systems and the way the human ear experiences sound, he became convinced that the problem was the manner in which the sound bounced off walls and other objects in a room before it reached his ear. It wasn't just the sound itself but rather the way the sound waves traveled. The map from the speaker to the listener, Amar realized, was wrong.

This was his solitary opening—a single idea for a small, fresh approach that balked tradition. He designed just one product, the 2201 model, which was a completely different type of speaker. It used a connected group of twenty-two small speakers pointed in different directions to simulate the impact and quality of a much larger system. This sole invention put Dr. Amar G. Bose on the map.

This is how Bose started small.

A novel approach to a speaker in 1964 wasn't exactly historical; if Bose had stopped there, his name wouldn't be synonymous today with high-quality audio. Rather than sitting back and enjoying the spoils from his one innovation, though, Bose used his small start to make history. Building off of his first product, he further refined the concept to launch the Bose 901 in 1968. This model became a commercial hit and is still manufactured today. The company expanded in the following decade and became the standard by which all others were measured.

Bose continued to start small as it released the industry's first custom-engineered automotive sound system in 1983 for several General Motors vehicles. A host of other products followed that leveraged the same opening Dr. Bose discovered when founding the company: the Bose noise-canceling headphones used by pilots and air travelers worldwide; the wireless Bose Mini, a small Bluetooth speaker that delivers concert-quality audio and is one of the most highly coveted accessories for smartphones of all types. Bose has a leadership position in home theater audio, commercial sound systems, musical amplification, PA systems, and even computer speakers. Bose systems have been used at the Olympics in Canada and France, and are the sound systems at the Sistine Chapel in Rome and the Great Mosque in Mecca. With over 11,000 employees and $3.4 billion in revenue, the Bose Corporation continues to exploit an innovation that was born from a frustrated grad student starting small.

## HILLARY HOOCH AND TRUMP TONIC

Starting small might seem easier when you're getting started—but what if you're already established? What if you've already got history and manufacturing and all of the overhead that comes with an established business? Figuring it out and finding a way is all well and good when you're young and have nothing to lose, but how can you really commit to uncharted territories when you've got mouths to feed?

That's the situation Avery's Beverages was facing. When Sherman Avery started making handcrafted soda in his red Connecticut barn back in 1904, he wasn't facing the crushing competitive pressure of industry giants like Coca-Cola and Pepsi. The root beer and ginger ale he made didn't need celebrity endorsements or Super Bowl halftime sponsorships; customers loved it based on the simplicity of good old-fashioned cane sugar and natural flavoring.

Over the years, the fierce marketplace of carbonated beverages became too much for this small-town producer. To make ends meet, the company started offering bottled water; by their centennial anniversary, five-gallon bottled water deliveries were the lion's share of revenue. While their quality had always been good, getting their products to stand out above the overwhelming competitive noise had become nearly impossible. Things were so bad that the company was strongly considering dropping the soda business altogether and just focusing on water.

For fun, in 2008, Avery Beverages tried a small experiment. In conjunction with the presidential election cycle, they produced a small batch of Barack O'Berry and John McCream sodas. The whimsical new offerings immediately sold out. Instead of chalking it up to good luck and buckling back down in the water business, the leaders at Avery saw this as their opening. They realized that fun-themed flavors and names could help garner publicity, customer attention, and sales. Linda's Smackdown Soda and Dick's Blue Menthol were sold during the 2010 Connecticut senate race between Republican Linda McMahon and Democrat Dick Blumenthal. Upon the news that Osama bin Laden had been killed in 2011, the company quickly launched So Long Osama, a blood orange soda.

They expanded the foothold they'd discovered by starting small with the launch of their Totally Gross Sodas. "Dedicated to the ten-year-old in all of us," flavors include Dog Drool, Bug Barf, Zombie BrainJuice, and Monster Mucus. These SODAsgusting® flavors became an instant hit among kids, college students, and curious adults. Swamp Juice, the first flavor in the series, "looks like bog water, but tastes like Skittles," according to Avery's operations manager Will Dunn.

Sales and excitement grew with the 2012 launch of Crème de Mitt, as Mitt Romney challenged Obama for the presidency. When the New England Patriots made headlines for "deflategate," Avery responded by launching Deflated Ball Brew. Today, the company is always on the lookout for topical and newsworthy ideas to inspire new flavors and names.

With the controversial 2016 presidential election, Avery enjoyed a 35 percent boost in revenue by launching fresh, new flavors dedicated to the candidates—Hillary Hooch, with the exact flavors listed as "classified," and Trump Tonic, an extra-acidic grape soda boasting the tagline "Make America Grape Again." Both flavors flew off the shelves and fueled Avery's growth and success. Even in the midst of a global pandemic, they brought back their limited-edition Trump Tonic, now opposed by the Biden Berry, for the 2020 election cycle. Starting small, Avery discovered a niche opening in themed beverages and then leveraged this approach to continuously expand their initial gain.

Albert Einstein once said, "We cannot solve our problems with the same thinking we used when we created them." As counterintuitive as starting small can seem in the "go big or go home" business environment, it can be a powerful tool for creative problem-solvers to disrupt existing assumptions and implement new approaches and strategies.

## START SMALL: TRY IT OUT

Although you can start small in almost any direction, training yourself to take this approach is so novel that it often takes extra effort. When you're used to making broad, sweeping changes, starting small can feel like not going far enough—or even standing still! Here are two exercises I've used with great success in both my own teams and with business leaders across multiple industries to instill the confidence to start small and immediately recognize the benefits.

## EXERCISE: PAIN-STORMING

While traditional brainstorming generates new ideas and approaches of all sizes, we often don't realize we're collecting great ideas for a misguided focus until it's too late. This is where pain-storming, uncovering the pain points suffered by your key customers and/or stakeholders, can help.

Instead of jumping to solutions, pain-storming uncovers the fundamental drivers of new opportunities, since "pain" is the source of problems waiting to be solved by new products, services, processes, and business models. It's a small start, shifting your perspective and focus, that often results in ideas for additional valuable small starts you can begin taking immediately.

1. Identify the specific person, customer, or stakeholder you're solving for.

2. Next, list out the specific steps and activities they go through when interacting with your product, service, or experience. What are the things they do, why, and to what end?

3. Compare that list to the intended use case of your product or service. What are they doing unnecessarily? What work-arounds have they created to modify your product or service to their needs? Is it different from the way things are "supposed" to be done?

4. Identify the biggest pain points that are the root causes of the customers' problems. This could be unmet needs or even desires for new features or benefits. What about your product or service causes them stress, concern, or dissatisfaction?

5. Use these pain points to identify new and unique solutions. Don't try to solve everything at once. Instead, start small and systematically knock out your customers' pain points one at a time.

## EXERCISE: CRAZY EIGHTS

Starting small doesn't have to mean going slow. This exercise, which originally comes from the world of design thinking, is a great way to eliminate the pressure points of starting small by leveraging time constraints. The goal is to generate as many ideas as possible within a short time frame—quantity, not quality.

1. Identify your target challenge, and give each participant a sheet of paper folded in half three times to make eight equally sized boxes.

2. Ask the group members to each sketch and describe a unique idea in each square so in the end you have eight new ideas. It's important to not only sketch your idea but to use words to describe what it is—this combination is highly effective in making abstract mental concepts more concrete on paper.

3. Give each participant no more than forty-five to sixty seconds for each square. Even if they're not complete, when it's time, move onto the next square.

4. Set a timer and go!

5. When the timer goes off, everyone must stop sketching and take a look at their ideas. Have each person choose their top three to present to the whole group.

6. When the group chooses their favorite three, give each participant a new sheet of paper folded into three sections.

7. Ask each participant to sketch out more details for these top three ideas, set the timer for six minutes, and go!

8. When the timer goes off, ask everyone to present their new sketches to the group and have each participant vote for their top two.

These chosen ideas can be submitted for another round of rapid sketching and voting to home in on even more details as many times as you'd like. At whatever point you feel you have the very best idea from the session, the team can start refining it as a group or working it up into a prototype.

## TACTIC 4

# START AT THE END

Stephen R. Covey's book *The Seven Habits of Highly Effective People* has sold over twenty-five million copies in forty languages since being published in 1989; it has been named by *Time* as one of the 25 Most Influential Business Management Books. People are often surprised, then, by the simplicity of the habits, particularly number two: begin with the end in mind. As Covey explains it:

> It's based on imagination—the ability to envision in your mind what you cannot at present see with your eyes. It is based on the principle that all things are created twice. There is a mental (first) creation, and a physical (second) creation. The physical creation follows the mental, just as a building follows a blueprint.

Creative problem-solvers are drawn to this analogy, but we also realize it's easier said than done.

Especially in more established organizations, most of our mental energy is spent on incremental changes to existing products, services, or processes. If you're the brand manager for Kellogg's Raisin Bran Crunch, it's much easier to consider changing from brown raisins to yellow ones than it is to ask a question like "What is the ideal breakfast our customers truly want?" And creative problem-solvers understand the effectiveness of these rapid experiments—if you've got a great product that people love, blowing it up every quarter isn't a solution to anything.

But certain problems we face are so big, so challenging, that figuring them out and finding a way is impossible at the tree level. When you need to see—or even create—the entire forest, starting at the end is an invaluable tool. If no solution seems possible or even desirable, begin with the vision of your ideal state and reverse engineer from there.

If you want to do something that's never been done, you probably need to go about it in a new way, too, so start at the finish line.

## START AT THE END IN ACTION

From making the impossible a tangible reality, to eliminating emotional attachments to solutions that don't work, to recognizing the right choice when every option looks ugly, these stories illustrate the effectiveness of figuring it out and finding a way by starting at the end.

### WHERE'S THE BEEF?

Picture this: Your mouth waters as you size up the sizzling, juicy burger on the plate in front of you. Charred top, juicy center, enchanting aroma—that first bite sends your taste buds into a state of pure bliss. Truly one of the best burgers you've ever tasted.

The catch? This "burger" is grown, not fed. Meet the Impossible Burger.

By starting at the end with exactly that vision, Stanford bio-chemist and entrepreneur Patrick Brown is now serving up an incredible burger substitute. Brown's company, Impossible Foods, has spent years working at the molecular level to craft the best darn plant-based burger in the world—so good, you won't even miss the real thing.

Making plants taste like a juicy burger is no small feat. Industry experts said it couldn't be done, sentencing healthy eaters to an endless stream of cardboard-flavored substitutes. But Brown knew he could crack the code. He wanted to protect the environment, help people live healthier lives, launch a successful company, and, of course, build one hell of a burger. "If people are going to be eating burgers in fifty years, they're not going to be made from cows," said Brown. "We're saving the burger."

With his eye squarely on the end product—that amazing, per-fect, "impossible" burger—Brown scientifically attacked every aspect, from the raw-to-cooked color change to the red juices that ooze out when pressed into a fresh bun. He reverse engineered a plant-based patty that is indistinguishable to the untrained eye . . . and mouth. His burger has more protein, fewer calories, and less fat than a traditional lean burger, while being much more ecologically sustainable.

Brown turned down Google's offer to buy the company for nearly $300 million since he feels his work to make the world a better place is still incomplete.

Too often we focus on the barriers, the roadblocks, and brick walls that hold us back, the zillion reasons that we can't achieve our vision. Even if we have the guts to chase a dream, it's easy to become dissuaded when facing early obstacles. For Brown, though, each setback simply fueled his commitment. He realized that every failed experiment was a step closer to an elegant solution. When you start with an end that everyone is convinced is impossible, you're not stymied by the failures. If there was a clear-cut path to the end result, your dream would already be on the table!

If Brown can convince carnivores that his plant products are as good as their beloved meat-based masterpieces, imagine what you can do by starting at the end when approaching your own challenges. If you have a clear vision (your compass) and you're unwilling to accept anything less than the end point you're working toward, even the seemingly impossible can become your reality.

## ROBOBEES

Do you realize that bees pollinate one in every three bites of food, providing 90 percent of the world's nutrition? Maurice Maeterlinck famously said, "If the bee disappeared from Earth, man would only have four years left to live." Alarmingly, the bee population—along with butterflies and other important pollinator insects—has been dropping precipitously, widely threatening global food supplies.

Starting at the end, the mission is clear: make more bees and save humanity!

The researchers at Harvard Microrobotics Lab knew the scope of the challenge (massive) and the barriers to solving it (numerous). While most people would try to solve a bee shortage by feeding, protecting, or breeding more actual bees, the Harvard team used an unconventional approach to solve the problem at hand. Rather than abandoning their considerable talents and resources and dedicating their lab space to starting new hives of bees that would face the same barriers, these researchers refused to accept that only bees could be bees. Utilizing their knowledge of unmanned aircraft (drones), they created a brand-new solution: RoboBees.

The RoboBee can lift off, hover to conserve energy, fly through dust, and swim. It flies faster than a real bee yet weighs less. In addition to conducting pollination missions, this tiny invention can ultimately expand to serve other purposes: "The RoboBees can eventually be used for search and rescue, for example, in areas where larger robots won't fit," says Harvard Microrobotics Laboratory researcher Elizabeth Helbling. "They would also return with the information faster, as you wouldn't have to wait for one robot to come back, but instead have a whole swarm of them covering a forest or similar."

By starting at the end and examining the desired results, this team has been able to look beyond the limitations and find uncharted territory to explore. Creative problem-solvers in love with the problem of saving humanity, they invented something new where others have only tried to double down on a failing solution. Starting at the end can be a valuable approach to clear away emotional responses and truly face the larger issues.

## WORKING OUT OF A BIND

Starting at the end is valuable for making fresh innovations and positive changes, but it's also an incredibly powerful approach when you're facing adversity. Creative problem-solvers start at the end and ask themselves questions like "Who will I be if I make this decision?" and "What will the world look like if we take this path?"

In the early 2000s, I was working at a digital promotions company called ePrize when our CEO instituted a company-wide bonus program. To align our team's efforts and give everyone a stake in the outcome, it was completely tied to the sales target; if we beat the $40 million target by a dollar, all three hundred people got a sizable bonus. If we missed it by a nickel, everyone got absolutely nothing.

We were all excited to be rewarded for our efforts to grow the company, and this initiative drove our behavior. Sacrifices were made, plans were crafted, and clients were wooed. Large digital scoreboards illuminated our offices across the country. This number was front and center for the entire company that year, and all of us were gunning hard to reach it.

On December 31, our CEO got the final tally and rushed to tell all of us: "We made it! We just got in the final order of the year and we reached $40,200,000. We hit the goal!"

Everyone was ecstatic. We patted ourselves on the back for all of our commitment, efforts, and hard work. Knowing our bonuses were coming in on February 15, a short forty-five days in the future, we all started placing deposits on summer vacations, ordering new furniture for our homes, and planning our financial lives accordingly.

Then on February 2, when our CFO discovered that we'd double counted one order and our grand total ended up around $39,970,000—just short—no one knew quite what to do. Legally, none of us was entitled to a single cent of bonus. Our CEO went to the board and explained the situation. In total, the bonuses added up to over $1 million. The board was clear in their position—better luck next year.

When the CEO gathered all of us into a team meeting, the mood was somber. We knew what was coming.

He talked about the soul-searching he'd had to do over the prior week, about the kind of company we were, the culture and philosophy that we stood for. He talked about our company commitment to results and how we'd never reach our collective goals by rewarding the misses.

And then he dropped the bombshell.

He told us that while results are paramount, the one thing that trumped performance was trust. He'd started from the end and played out each scenario in his mind. If he didn't pay the bonus and saved a million dollars, he'd undermine the trust he'd built with us over the last seven years. He'd determined he'd lose more than that amount in the form of apathy, employee attrition, broken trust, and damaged morale. An investment in our team and culture was better than the penalty tax of perceived betrayal. He knew he couldn't expect people to run through fires for him if he wasn't willing to do the same in return.

He announced that the bonuses were going to be paid. In full. Every penny. On time.

The room exploded; some of us laughed, while others cried.

That enthusiasm carried forward long after the meeting ended. Morale was sky-high, turnover was low, and we overdelivered as a family. Based on our CEO's demonstration of trust and commitment, the team rallied and paid it back. The story became known in the community and was often repeated to us by new people applying for jobs. I'm convinced that our CEO's million-dollar payout that day was one of the best investments he ever made. The normal linear decision process of moving from one square to the next would have led to a cash savings and a shattered team. By starting at the end, clearly identifying the company he wanted to be, he was able to reason through, make the right call, turn a difficult situation into a positive one, and ultimately create the most possible value.

It's not an accident that, several years and several companies later, I cofounded Platypus Labs with him. Yes, I'm still working with that incredible CEO, Josh Linkner, today.

## DON'T KNOW SHIT FROM SHINOLA

This familiar phrase became popular in the 1940s, during the rapid growth of American industrialism. Nothing was more patriotic than making something by hand right here in the US of A. As globalization shifted the economic landscape in the decades that followed, the notion of locally handcrafted goods—and American manufacturing—became a quaint relic of the past. The actual product from the saying, Shinola shoe polish, went out of business in 1960.

Tom Kartsotis knows all about global goods. He founded Overseas Products in 1984 on the premise that Americans would love the fashionable watches he could import from Hong Kong, and they did. Today, the company, renamed Fossil, boasts over $3 billion in revenue and employs over ten thousand people worldwide.

After selling the company, Tom had a wacky new vision: an upscale, handcrafted watch—made in America. Despite a crowded market dominated by foreign manufacturers, in which the last major all-American companies had packed up shop half a century ago, he wanted to create a product that would represent quality crafts-manship and national pride. He believed customers would also be enamored by the nostalgic connection to American manufacturing.

Kartsotis could've started with his previous experience and contacts in the watch business and built up from there. Instead, he started at the end and reverse engineered his ideal state.

It started with his brand name. He could have cooked up a new name, just like he did with Fossil. But he sought to license the name of an iconic brand that represented the heyday of American manufacturing. The defunct Shinola Shoe Polish Company was a brand name that everyone knew, a connection to the past. The name already conveyed a sense of humor, a head-tilting curiosity, and the implication that it could be something other than what's expected.

Now, he needed to choose just the right location to craft these watches. Starting at the end, he assembled focus groups to get cus-tomer feedback on different hometowns. He tried Shinola, USA. He tested Shinola, Los Angeles. There was a Shinola, Chicago, test. But when he tested Shinola, Detroit, the results were off the charts. The "brand" of Detroit perfectly connected with the vibe he was trying to create. It was a symbol of grit and determination, of American ingenuity. Detroit had fallen on hard times and was fighting hard for a rebirth. With the end goal in mind, Kartsotis knew that Detroit could help Shinola, and Shinola could help Detroit.

The Shinola team had a strong vision of what these watches would look like in the end, but it was a tricky combination of grit and luxury. For the luxury element, their research revealed that the best way to start building watches would be to bring in the highest-quality components from Switzerland. For the grit, well, Shinola hadn't just chosen Detroit because of its public image; the Motor City is also the home of the automobile, the moving assembly line, and of many highly skilled former factory workers who were looking for jobs. Shinola brought together the existing skill set of this pool of workers with the training and luxury components that would allow them to assemble beautiful precision timepieces.

The Shinola team now crafts upscale bicycles, leather goods, and, of course, watches. In the digital and disposable age, Shinola's high-quality and simple design stand out. Today, you may spot a Shinola on the arm of President Obama or any number of public figures (president Bill Clinton bought fourteen), and the brand is featured in high-end retailers like Nordstrom, Saks Fifth Avenue, and Barney's New York. Customers don't just wear a Shinola because it looks nice or is high quality but because they like what it says about them. The watch represents tenacity and resilience, simplicity and durability. Tom didn't just build a watch company—he built a luxury American lifestyle brand.

Starting at the end, the Shinola team reverse engineered their approach, first establishing their desired outcome of being an American manufacturer with the cache of the past. Only then did they begin charting their course. In fact, Kartsotis is still working toward the all-American-made watch; by starting at the end, though, now he has a respected brand, highly skilled team, and nationwide support working on it with him.

Think about how you and your team navigate the work in your own organization. Do people require detailed, step-by-step instructions? Is every move and every moment accounted for? What happens when you're facing a novel issue, or when you don't want the result you know you can expect from the options available? How do you expect to create something the world has never seen without making room for creativity?

Management by operating manuals worked fine when markets were local, customers were homogenous, product cycles occurred over decades, and complexity was minimal. The cost to produce those manuals, those maps, may have been justified since change was slow. Workers—and frankly, most leaders—didn't need to think all that much on their own. Following the path would ensure safe arrival at a safe destination.

But we now face rapidly proliferating change—and if we want to change the world and make the impossible happen, we need to create even more change. Imagine the difficulty of creating a street map if the roadways completely shifted five times an hour! Imagine navigating an expedition to Mars staring at a map of Brooklyn!

When organizations simply follow the corporate GPS, progress shrivels. Creative problem-solvers figure it out by embracing the compasses over maps mindset, and they empower their employees to do the same. Provide a clear vision of your destination point, and give your team the tools to navigate their own paths. Encourage them to make their own informed decisions and start small in the face of ambiguity. Give them the target and resources, then let them use their ingenuity and judgment to find the best route.

## START AT THE END: TRY IT OUT

Muhammad Ali attributed becoming the heavyweight champion to a single fact that he often repeated: "I am the greatest."

The best of the best in every field, from athletes to actors to business moguls, often cite the mental practices they diligently employ to enhance their performances. From vision boards to affirmations to mental rehearsals, visualization starts at the end and creates a confluence of mind, body, and action. Creative problem-solvers can use these same techniques to figure it out and find a way to their own incredible, world-changing results.

## EXERCISE: THE MAGAZINE COVER

The goal is to visualize what the future looks like—what the landscape will be *after* you crack and implement the code—so you can work backward and pinpoint the actions you need to take.

Take one situation you're facing; instead of digging yourself out of the hole one step at a time, imagine the obstacle completely eliminated. In fact, you've just landed on the cover of *Harvard Business Review* for your brilliant, creative solution.

1. Draw the magazine cover. What is the headline and support-ing copy?

2. What is the key image that communicates your core strategy and success factors?

3. Provide an executive summary—why did you win? In what new ways did you leverage technology? How are you differ-entiating yourself from your competitors? What are your customers saying about your innovative solution?

4. Now, work backwards to where you are today. What was the last step before completion? What about the step before that? What resources did you utilize? What about the step before that?

## EXERCISE: THE WORLD'S FIRST

If you're going to take an uncharted path, you're going to discover something brand new. In this exercise, you're only allowed to share ideas that begin with "the world's first." Starting at the end, you envision a new product or service that the world has never seen. It could be the world's first insurance policy for drones. Or the world's first 3D-printed burger joint. It doesn't have to be earth-shattering—what about the world's first hotel that offers guests a warm chocolate chip cookie upon arrival? The DoubleTree Hotel credits that simple idea for differentiating them in a crowded market and helping them succeed. Big or small, brainstorming the world's first will push your creativity to new heights and help you unlock bold possibilities.

## EXERCISE: THE TIME MACHINE

As interesting as it is to visualize starting at the end, it's fascinating to recognize that where you are and what you're doing at this very moment is all of your yesterdays' end. Imagine you have a time machine: if you could go back and visit yourself ten years in the past, what are three game-changing things you are doing now that you would gift your past self?

On the flip side, if you go ten years into the future, what are three game-changing ideas that you would bring back and apply to your current challenges or opportunities?

# NOTHING IS STATIC

Many of you know about Blockbuster's demise, but did you know that they had multiple opportunities to buy Netflix?

In 2000, Netflix proposed that they would handle Blockbuster's online component; in return, Blockbuster would host its in-store component, thus eliminating the need for mailed DVDs. According to an interview with former Netflix CFO Barry McCarthy, "They just about laughed us out of their office."

It's a far-too-common story: once-great leaders and organizations become intoxicated by their own successes. They are unable to let go of the past. They fail to adapt, fail to innovate, and then they simply fail. In the *Harvard Business Review*, Martin Reeves, author of *Your Strategy Needs Strategy*, defines the "success trap" as "companies that over-exploit their current business models and fail to explore future growth opportunities." From Blockbuster Video to Compaq, PanAm Airlines to Oldsmobile, the success trap has killed hundreds of previous market leaders. For most of us in the business world, this is common sense, even cliché. Common sense, unfortunately, is not always common practice. Leaders fail, and more often than we'd like to think.

Why don't more organizations embrace creative problem-solving as a long-term strategy? "Most follow a path toward lower exploration and risk falling into the success trap," explains Reeves:

Paradoxically, doing so often seems like the right choice. Fine-tuning the established, successful model provides higher immediate rewards at low risk. Over a five-year period, one in three companies make that mistake. This comes at the cost of lower growth, which jeopardizes the company's future. Fast forward a few years, and lower growth means fewer interactions with new, demanding customer groups and less inspiration to innovate. Eventually the company is likely to be out of touch with changing market requirements. At that point, it is often too late to course-correct.

Once in the trap, it is difficult to escape: seven out of ten fail to leave it in the next five years and get back onto the path of higher exploration.

## BE *FROGGER*

Traditional approaches to creative problem-solving are simply out of date; friction-free global markets fueled by fully transparent, real-time information have commoditized previous competitive advantages.

Growing up in an era when video games hit the mainstream, I was always drawn to the arcades in Tokyo, where I'd play games such as *Galaga*, *Astroids*, *Dig Dug*, and *Space Invaders* for hours. My favorite game, however, was *Frogger*.

Do you remember it? You assume the role of a motivated frog trying to make your way across a river. Without the ability to swim, you must hop on logs, turtles, and lily pads as they glide past. The challenge is that nothing remains stationary. Each leap onto stable ground is temporary, since all the items are zooming down the river. If you try to stay on stable footing too long, you fall into the river—game over. To win, you must leap quickly from one short-lived success to another. As the game advances, safe harbors become less frequent and faster moving, leaving the poor frog in a constant state of unrest and instability.

Sound familiar?

To a great degree, we are living in a three-dimensional game of *Frogger*. Competitive wins, top-tier financial performance, and brand supremacy are all temporary states met with an ever-increasing stream of change. Nothing is static.

Yet the models we use to lead, innovate, and grow have not evolved to meet the challenges of the day. Traditionalist approaches are yielding diminishing returns as the playing field becomes more complex and difficult. While most of us fall back on our instincts of doubling down on what worked in the past, those embracing these mindsets of creative problem-solvers will enjoy a disproportionate share of the spoils.

Creative problem-solvers understand that the only constant must be our ability to learn, grow, and adapt. They understand that innovation is a continuous process, not a once-a-decade initiative. Embracing this mindset is no longer optional; it has become mission critical to sustainable success.

The knowledge that nothing is static is your primary weapon to fight this trend toward complacency. We have to be willing to let go of the ways of the past, to challenge current assumptions, to lean into what's next. It's the recognition that we can no longer rely on models of the past to help us drive the growth and success we look for in the future.

This mindset isn't about fearmongering but maintaining a constant thirst for knowledge and self-improvement. Complacency is simply not an option. Embrace, don't fear, change. Constantly initiate it—actively court and choose it—instead of running from it or waiting for someone else to corner you into it. From systems to solutions, nothing lasts forever, so relish learning, growing, and exploring new possibilities.

## Beliefs

- Knowledge and ability must never be stationary.

- Adapting quickly is paramount.

- Speed wins.

- Every system is in a constant state of flux.

- Complacency is poisonous.

- Yesterday's solution is today's trash.

## Characteristics

- Craves learning

- Embraces rapid change

- Comfortable letting go of previous notions

- Forward looking

- Commits to continuous improvement

## Tactics

- The judo flip

- The mash-up

## TACTIC 5

# THE JUDO FLIP

If nothing is static, everything is in flux, and none of the standard go-to solutions are working, how *should* you solve a problem?

Do the opposite.

Judo flipping is all about doing the exact opposite of what's expected. Whether it's flipping your first inclination upside down or following that inkling when it's the opposite of what you're *supposed* to do, this strategy is all about thumbing your nose at expectations and daring to do things totally differently. Judo flip a tradition; judo flip a process; judo flip a threat. This type of oppositional thinking has fueled innovation since the start of time and is the hallmark of creative problem-solvers. The judo flip is a powerful framework to unlock fresh ideas and foster innovation.

To deploy the judo flip against your own challenge, force yourself to explore the complete opposite of what's always been done. When facing a challenge or new opportunity, make a list of how all the "experts" would generally attack it. Make a list of what you've done in the past, what your mentors did, what the industry norms are, and how everyone else goes about facing the same issue. Then draw a line down the page and force yourself to imagine the *exact* opposite of each of those approaches. The exact opposite isn't necessarily the innovation you're looking for—it's just the opposite. But it'll provide the spark of creativity you need to creatively solve the problem at hand.

In nearly every field, the industry stalwarts long for days gone by and refuse to consider fresh approaches. Even the most creative problem-solver is in grave danger of being upended if we always zig and never even consider the zag. No matter how staid your profession may be, judo flipping may be instrumental to your very survival.

## THE JUDO FLIP IN ACTION

Judo flipping is, by its very nature, a thrill. From literal flips to throwing out the rule book, the following examples are from creative problem-solvers who have embraced that roller-coaster sensation and defied gravity and common wisdom to make history.

## CREATIVE CANNONBALLS

Kevin Bull was already a successful stock trader and entrepreneur by the time he finally earned a shot to compete as a walk-on for *American Ninja Warrior*. On national TV, surrounded by contestants who were more athletic, more experienced, and better prepared, he stared down Cannonball Alley, the eighth obstacle in the Venice City Finals.

It was a formidable challenge: three heavy, dodgeball-sized cannonballs suspended by ropes over a large pool of water. The objective was to make it from one side to the other by grabbing one swinging cannonball and leaping to the next without falling in the water. Sixteen of the world's best athletes had attempted it before Bull, and all sixteen of them had failed. The enormous upper body strength they'd built and relied on had been too severely depleted by the first seven obstacles. The odds were simply not in Bull's favor.

Creative innovators are innately curious, refusing to accept conventional approaches or established practices as the only routes to success. So Bull, who lacked the raw power and raw strength of those who'd failed before him, knew he needed a different approach—he needed a judo flip. While other competitors had assumed the only way to conquer the dreaded Cannonball Alley was to increase upper-body strength, Kevin's unorthodox flip would make headlines.

After clearing the first two balls and moving to the third—the place where so many others had failed—Kevin stunned the crowd by literally flipping his body upside down and grabbing the last hanging cannonball with his legs. Though his upper-body strength had deteriorated from intense overuse, his fresh legs were able to grasp the target. Kevin locked his legs around the ball and swung his body toward the finish line. He leaped in midair to land on his feet on the dry platform, and spectators matched his leap, screaming with both approval and astonishment as this unlikely ninja became the first man to triumph Cannonball Alley.

Kevin Bull literally and figuratively flipped traditional thinking upside down in order to win.

## MIDMOUNTAIN FLIPS

Most companies do whatever they can to protect their portion of the market. Smart companies innovate so *they* can be the source of disruption, rather than being disrupted. What kind of company tells their own customers to stop buying their own best-selling, core product?

That type of oppositional thinking is next-level, creative problem-solving judo flipping in action. And it's just what Chouinard Equipment did in 1972.

Yvon Chouinard had been an avid climber since his early teenage years, often living for extended periods of time in national parks. He and his friends idolized the likes of great American naturalists Henry David Thoreau and John Muir. To support himself, Chouinard began making some of his own climbing equipment, specifically pitons. Pitons are hard metal spikes that are hammered into a mountain to aid in climbing, then forcibly removed afterward.

Chouinard was inspired after meeting dedicated climber John Salathé, who made pitons from the axles of old Model A cars. In order to make pitons from scrap metal, Chouinard taught himself blacksmithing. After years of peddling his pitons from the back of his car, demand increased enough for Chouinard to partner up with fellow climber Tom Frost to form Chouinard Equipment in 1965. They continuously evolved pitons and other climbing equipment, utilizing a design principle borrowed from French aviator and author Antoine de Saint Exupéry: "Perfection is finally attained not when there is no longer anything to add, but when there is no longer anything to take away."

Five years later, they were the largest supplier of climbing hardware in America. And that was a problem.

These dedicated outdoorsmen, committed to enjoying and preserving nature, realized their main product, the piton, was decimating the landscapes they most loved. As climbing gained in popularity, well-traveled mountain passes began to show the destruction from each climber's pitons being hammered in and scraped out.

So, in their first catalog in 1972, Chouinard Equipment pulled a legendary judo flip. Their catalog opened with a full editorial explaining the detrimental effect of pitons on the landscape. Everyone needed to stop using—and buying—pitons immediately. They'd tossed their own biggest product in the trash.

They were prepared, though. Before launching the catalog, they'd developed a brand-new product: chocks. Chocks leave no trace of a climber; they are reusable; they preserve the beauty of the climb for the next adventurer.

It worked. Within a few months, demand for pitons dried up, and chocks were flying out the door.

The following year, Chouinard Equipment began expanding into outdoor clothing and decided to split the company. Chouinard Equipment remained the go-to for climbing hardware, but the clothing was their own brand: Patagonia.

By 1985, Patagonia's garments, mostly constructed of polypropylene and bunting, were a beloved mainstay for climbers and campers alike. But they'd been experimenting with two new fabrics, Capilene polyester and Synchilla fleece, and they were positive that they'd be more durable. Rather than slowly rolling out new garments in the new fabrics, they judo flipped again and replaced all their polypropylene and bunting—70 percent of their sales—in one fell swoop. They believed in their new products and believed in their customers, and the strategy paid off yet again.

After learning that the pesticides used on cotton were environmentally detrimental, in the fall of 1994, they committed to making their cotton sportswear 100 percent organic within eighteen months. Yes, in another judo flip, they decided to wage war on conventional cotton—on a significant portion of their supply chain.

Of course, they had committed to the impossible. The infrastructure for organic cotton wasn't ready for that volume; the brokers simply didn't have it to sell. But they worked back from their desired outcome through organic certifiers, spinners, and ginners to figure out how to get them to accommodate the needs of this project. They found farmers and gained their commitment to utilize organic methods, long before such a thing became standard fare.

Although industry experts lambasted Patagonia's ambitions, these creative problem-solvers made their deadline. Every piece of cotton Patagonia clothing has been 100 percent organic cotton since 1996.

Patagonia has shown the ethical and financial benefits possible for both creative problem-solving and sustainability. With an understanding that nothing is static, they judo flipped major portions of their business to ensure that they really are the change they want to see in the world. They set the bar for big companies to commit to real environmental changes and show that doing so can be satisfying and very profitable.

## THE WONKAVATOR

When it comes down to it, the modern elevator industry hasn't changed much since Elisha Otis pioneered it back in 1845. Sure, the cars are faster, there are some digital displays, and the doors automatically open and shut now, but the essential concept is the same. An elevator, fundamentally, propels riders up and down a single shaft on a cable pulley system. It's a human dumbwaiter.

Despite the company currently owning 12.2 percent of the worldwide elevator market, the quintessential definition just didn't satisfy the talented, creative problem-solvers at German industrial conglomerate ThyssenKrupp. What if they could create a system that moved in multiple directions? What if there were no cables? What if a single shaft could transport multiple cabins? What if elevators could not only go up and down but side to side? It could expand the uses of elevators completely and offer a new form of transportation altogether.

Rejecting the established path, they've judo flipped the cable-driven elevator industry. By inventing magnetic-levitation technology, they've created an elevator car that can travel with no cables at all. This breakthrough allows for the previously impossible, such as multiple cars sharing the same shaft, vertical *and* horizontal travel, and even integration with other means of transportation, like movable walkways or subway systems. It could liberate architects, who currently design buildings around core elevator shafts, to create new, unrestricted designs. It is also poised to offer a significant cost savings to construction companies and building operators.

The new technology represents the single biggest elevator breakthrough in over 160 years. Called the Multi, the first full-scale system is currently being installed in OVG Real Estate's new East Side Tower Building in Berlin.

These engineers shattered conventional wisdom by challenging the very foundation of their field. It was a "given" that all elevators operate with a shaft-and-cable system, like a giant yo-yo carrying passengers. Judo flipping this set belief allowed the team to explore new options and discover fresh possibilities.

## BUT HOW SHOULD IT BE?

Creative problem-solvers judo flip themselves, their products, their cultures, and their industries despite often being initially ridiculed for their game-changing ideas. But there's one industry I can think of that seems to be in a constant state of judo flipping one-upmanship—and from the consumer side, I think we're all relieved.

Do you remember getting your first car? Talk about a rite of passage, a passport to freedom, a thrill so huge it completely suspends disbelief. Entire textbooks have been written about the American love affair with the car—but I've never seen one about the American love affair with the car dealership. For every aspiring engineer, auto mechanic, and teenager jumping through hoops to get their license, I can't recall anyone who relished the idea of spending time at the dealership—even the dealers themselves.

Why? Well, let's draw out the conventional and quintessential car dealership model:

| CONVENTIONAL CAR DEALER |
| --- |
| Sells one brand of car |
| Hours: 8 a.m.–6 p.m., Monday through Friday |
| Drive off the lot |
| Once you buy it, it's yours |
| Local |
| Paperwork at dealer |
| Haggling salesperson |
| All cars sold from dealer |
| Cars, parts, and repairs |
| Slow career growth |

It's no conventional DMV, but it's not exactly Disneyland, either.

Now let's draw a line down the middle and see what the judo flips might look like:

| CONVENTIONAL WISDOM | JUDO FLIP |
| --- | --- |
| Hours: 8 a.m.–6 p.m., Monday through Friday | 24-7 |
| Drive off the lot | Home delivery |
| Once you buy it, it's yours | Twenty-one-day risk-free trial |
| Local | National |
| Paperwork at dealer | Digital docs via your mobile device |
| Haggling salesperson | Dealers bid for your pricing |
| All cars sold from dealer | Facilitate peer-to-peer deals |
| Cars, parts, and repairs | Many additional offerings (travel, insurance, apparel, etc.) |

These judo flips enabled AutoNation to shake up the dealership business. Launched as the first national dealership offering dozens of brands, no-haggle pricing, and expanded hours, the company became the most successful car dealership in history. They recently sold their twelve millionth car (no other dealership is even close), employ twenty-six thousand people, and have a market value of over $5 billion on the New York Stock Exchange.

Their success has caused a domino effect in the industry—now every entrant aims for bigger and more exciting judo flips, much to the benefit of the consumer.

Carvana, a "dealership-free car buying experience," challenges every aspect of the car-buying process. The online search engine they developed is now widely employed, allowing customers to browse cars from their own living rooms, using advanced features combined with virtual tours. As customers narrow their car search down to a few finalists, they can easily compare and contrast the respective features to make the best decision. The cars, which are all "Carvana Certified," pass a 150-point inspection to provide peace of mind for buyers. Once a decision is made, buyers complete the entire process, financing, and all the paperwork online quickly (current record is eleven minutes). And here's the really cool part: when it comes time to pick up your new ride, you visit the world's first car vending machines. Imagine those Matchbox car garages you played with as a kid. You walk up to a glass structure the size of a large building, enter a code, and one of dozens of garage doors opens . . . the one containing your new car. Hop in and drive off, no glad-handing required.

Car manufacturers, challenged by this lack of brand loyalty, have started to realize they can no longer rely on the dealership experience that served them so well. Now, to reach the consumer, they're putting in the extra effort to woo them with their own experiences. The Porsche Passport subscription plan is a great example of this. Rather than throwing money into a single car that starts depreciating the moment you drive it off the lot, with a monthly fee, you buy access into Porsche's entire fleet. Want to speed down the road with the top down in a 911 on Tuesday but need something Cayenne-sized for a family outing on Friday? No problem, just request your next car through the Passport app. Here, there are no acquisition, maintenance, or disposition costs—they're all included in your monthly fee. You're not buying a single car—you're buying the Porsche experience, and they've made that experience as mutable as your needs. The model has been so successful in pilot that other manufacturers have started exploring their own options, including Book by Cadillac and Harley Davidson's EaglerRider Club.

Judo flipped by creative problem-solvers, the entire car-buying experience has been upended to save customers money, provide better choices, ease the process, and create a (more pleasantly) memorable experience. All the while, these companies are more profitable than the typical dealerships staffed with salespeople and a support team.

## THE JUDO FLIP: TRY IT OUT

Whether you're staring down a pesky problem or just itching to shake up the status quo, it's time to apply some judo-flip logic.

Instead of seeking incremental solutions or looking at how others currently solve similar challenges, ask what would happen if you completely flipped the problem upside down. Think about conventional approaches—the way you've always done it—and then flip them upside down in order to yield better results.

1. Make a list of the sacred beliefs and assumptions that are part of your product, service, process, or experience. This is a list of the way things currently get done.

2. Next, judo flip each item; write the polar opposite. Note that the opposite is not necessarily the innovation—it's just the opposite.

3. Next, look at the list of opposites, and use it as inspiration to discover fresh, new approaches to tackle your challenge. Remember that you're not looking for a finished work product here but rather sparks of creativity that can be nurtured and adapted into fresh approaches or innovative breakthroughs.

4. As you practice this technique, create your own mantra—"Flip it," "Reverse it," "Do the opposite." It could be spoken, displayed in a mobile app, written on index cards, printed on signs in conference rooms, or included in your company's email signature. Whatever you do, make it your own—and ingrain oppositional thinking as a core tenet of your business philosophy to help you uncover creative approaches to solving complex problems.

# THE JUDO FLIP WORKSHEET

| STEP 1 | STEP 2 | STEP 3 |
|--------|--------|--------|
| Write down the rules and assumptions that are part of the product, process, or experience you're working on. | Next, Judo Flip it! What is the opposite? Remember, the opposite is NOT necessarily the innovation, it's just the opposite. | Then, use the list of opposites to ideate new and unique solutions to tackle your challenge or opportunity. |
|  |  |  |

# TACTIC 6

# THE MASH-UP

Creative problem-solvers know that nothing is static—that the best, strongest, most beloved product, company, or process will someday be a relic. At Platypus Labs, we always say, "Someday, a company will come along and put us out of business—it might as well be us!"

The mash-up is all about combining seemingly disparate items to help creatively solve the problem at hand. It's about combining one approach with another to undercover a fresh, potentially more effective option.

Combining two ingredients to create a brand-new substance has been a source of innovation for many of our favorite things—products, services, recreational activities, music, medical advances, and culinary delights. A bed combined with a chair to form the La-Z-Boy recliner. The smash Broadway hit *Hamilton* fused American history with hip-hop and other musical genres to rake in twelve Tony Awards in a highly competitive industry. Sometimes the best solution isn't a new one but existing solutions combined and reimagined.

When you're facing an innovation challenge of your own, experiment not only with individual solutions but also with mashing up existing concepts to uncover novel solutions. Here, your role is "fusion artist"—mashing two or more concepts together to create something entirely new. Maybe you combine two strategies into one; maybe you take one of your strategies and combine it with something from another industry. The result is one elegant solution you can't imagine having lived without.

# THE MASH-UP IN ACTION

The beauty with the mash-up is in the teams it creates. Whether they've whipped together new foods for us to enjoy, brought together disparate skill sets and expertise, or created new experiences by mashing up their offerings, the creative problem-solvers in these examples have proved, *Captain Planet*–style, that their forces combined make great things even better.

## LIKE PEANUT BUTTER AND . . .

"You got your peanut butter in my chocolate," an actor protests.

"No! You got your chocolate in my peanut butter," another angrily retorts.

"Delicious!" they both proclaim in unison upon trying the newly formed Reese's Peanut Butter Cup.

Since the company's launching in 1928, the basic Reese's concept has been combined with many other things to form several notable associations—fused with a corn puff, it makes cereal; fused with ice cream and the most ubiquitous food chain in the world, it makes a McFlurry. The company currently offers nineteen Reese's products, from sandwich spread to snack mix, and has licensed its brand and recipe to dozens of other manufacturers. One delicious association just leads to another and another.

Every recipe is a literal example of the mash-up, so it's not surprising that there are so many examples from the food industry. One really sticks out for me, though, as real reinvention and competitive differentiator.

There are few industries more fiercely competitive than fast food. With over $200 billion in revenue and 250,000 locations in the United States alone, this is one supersized industry, but it also faces deep challenges, including razor-thin margins, complex supply chains, and a highly transient workforce. A slight advantage could yield millions in profit, while a setback can send stock prices tumbling. In the last three years alone, McDonald's stock price has yo-yoed up and down, sending the market cap down by over $20 billion from high points and then back up again.

Fighting to stay competitive in a burger-dominated industry, Taco Bell CEO Greg Creed challenged his team to reinvent the crunchy taco, the company's fifty-year-old staple. Considering hundreds of ideas, ranging from different ingredients to bold new packaging, the one that got the team excited was the association of a Doritos chip with the classic Taco Bell mainstay. This mash-up is known as the Doritos Locos Taco, and it became a gigantic hit. In the first year, over six hundred million units were sold, generating extraspicy profits for both Taco Bell and FritoLay (the owner of Doritos), who had joined forces for the launch. It has gone on to become one of the most successful products in fast-food history. In the highly competitive fast-food arena, Taco Bell is standing out by mashing it up.

## IMPREZIVE

Ádám Somlai-Fischer trained as an architect before expanding his work as an artist; as he started to gain international acclaim, he was often asked to present his work to audiences. That's where he hit a roadblock. His ideas made the most impact when he could show the audience the big picture, then drill into the relationships between one concept and another—the lower-level bathroom needed to be understood in the context of the adjacent family room to fully understand the space—but PowerPoint, Keynote, and every other available presentation software were based on linear, page-after-page approaches.

Rather than subject his audiences to a jumbled slideshow that couldn't convey the concepts, Ádám decided to cobble together an alternative. Using an artist's canvas, then zooming in and out of concepts with cameras to show relationships and detail, he was able to finally communicate in the way he wanted—and despite the crude clunkiness of his tools, audiences went wild.

Péter Halácsy, a computer science professor and software developer, happened to see one of Ádám's homemade presentations, and as interested as he was in the ideas, he was even more intrigued by the potential for this nonlinear approach to storytelling. After the talk, Péter approached Ádám and suggested they collaborate to take the idea of a canvas-based zooming presentation and turn it into simple software that could be used by others. The two began working around the clock to build a whole new kind of presentation tool. This association between the artist and the programmer created the zoomable user interface (ZUI).

At the early prototype stage, Ádám and Péter were both excited by the potential but realized that they didn't have any business skills; the ZUI was born, but how would they get it into the hands of anyone else to use? They turned to Peter Arvai, a proved entrepreneur who had the skills and experience to build a company.

For the next eighteen months, this haphazard trio toiled away, spending 100 percent of their energy for zero pay. They set out to build a software application that could be used by millions to tell better, more memorable stories, to build a company that could scale, one that would help put their home of Budapest on the map as a birthplace of great start-ups.

In the presentation software space today, there are four major players: Microsoft, Apple, Google, and . . . Prezi. Prezi's 100 million customers have created over 360 million presentations, and the association of these three men created a small Hungarian start-up that has defied the underpinnings of what presentation tools can and should be.

It turns out ZUI isn't just cool—it is more effective. Brain science studies show that humans learn and retain more information when they understand the spatial relationship between concepts. Don't believe me? Let me walk you through the simple experiment Peter Arvai ran on us here at Platypus Labs when we had the opportunity to sit down with him: name your five favorite kitchen appliances.

After we rattled off our answers—stove, toaster, espresso machine, and so on—Peter chuckled. "So, how did you come up with the items? You probably did a mental walk-through in your own kitchen, right? You didn't envision a bullet point list." We all nodded as he explained that the relative location of one item to another is critical in human comprehension: "Those visual cues make for much stronger learning. Which is why audience retention rates are 30 percent or higher when Prezi is used over PowerPoint."

The company continues to gain ground against their Herculean competitors by staying connected to their sense of purpose: "We want to empower people to share ideas in better ways." This big vision that fuels the team was brought to life by a series of mash-ups—of ideas and people, technology and culture, art and science. Their initial mash-up has helped them attract $72 million in capital, disrupt the sleeping giants, and enable better communications.

## SHOPPING YOUR CLOSET

The best of the best used to only need to be great at one thing. The most luxurious hotels in the world, when you drilled down to it, just needed to provide shelter for guests. The most upscale department stores just needed to provide high-quality clothing and goods for their customers. But as we've all become more pressed for time and every option imaginable is just a click away, many consumers expect more from former one-trick ponies. When we're paying for the best, we expect to be wowed by fresh ideas and curated solutions.

In an effort to better serve their high-end customers and differentiate themselves from their competitors, the St. Regis Hotel in Washington, DC, partnered with luxury retailer Neiman Marcus to create one haute mash-up. Before guests arrive at the five-star hotel, they are asked to complete a quick online survey about their fashion styles, sizes, and who will be staying in the room. Upon arrival, guests discover a fully stocked closet, courtesy of Neiman Marcus, hand selected according to the survey results. I may find a Hugo Boss suit that I didn't even realize would be exactly the outfit

I needed to make a big impression during my meeting; a female exec may discover a gorgeous new pair of Jimmy Choo pumps in her size and favorite color. Fusing fashion and retail with luxury travel, the novel concept makes it easy for customers to discover new wares. They are welcome to try it all on and then just keep what they want. Upon checkout, any items that are removed by the guests are automatically billed to their master account.

One of the most fascinating aspects of this mash-up is that it was born out of a completely empty space: when marketers started looking around their hotels' rooms to find where they could create more value and impact for their customers. By not only filling the closet but partnering with another industry, they activated potential out of thin air! Neither luxury hotels nor expensive fashion retail is a new concept, but the intersection of the two creates a unique and compelling option for customers: in-suite customized apparel shopping. When mashed up together, it's a powerful approach to discovery, innovation, and progress.

As you tackle your own challenges and opportunities, consider the many ways that the mash-up can be deployed to fight not only novel problems but the sheer force of entropy on your industry. Here are just a few more examples of how mixing together various elements that already existed created fresh, innovative blends:

- **RELATED CONCEPTS:** Combine professional boxing with martial arts, and you get a brand-new sport: MMA (Mixed Martial Arts). Over the last decade, MMA has taken off as a premier sport, drawing fans from 156 countries. The UFC league was purchased in 2016 by talent conglomerate WME for $4 billion.

- **EMERGING TRENDS:** 1) An aging population, 2) increasingly comfortable with online shopping, 3) which also requires an increasingly complex and complicated routine of daily meds and vitamins—mashing up these three trends led TJ Parker to invent PillPack, an online pharmacy that delivers individual per-dosage packets of patients' medications instead of single-drug bottles. Since its conception at a 2012 MIT medical hackathon, PillPack has been licensed in all fifty states, employs over five hundred people, and was purchased in 2018 for $753 million by Amazon.

- **CUSTOMER EXPERIENCE:** What happens if you combine golf, competitive video games, and a modern luxury entertainment venue? TopGolf. Visitors rent out luxury suites tricked out with food, drinks, and comfy couches, stepping outside only to enjoy their own unparalleled driving range. Using their favorite clubs, players whack balls not only for distance but to earn points and rewards in a giant video game–like experience. Over thirteen million people have visited one of more than fifty TopGolf venues, and this hot mash-up continues to expand into new markets.

- **GEOGRAPHIC PREFERENCES:** African rhythms and European harmonies were among the elements blended to create a unique new style of American music: jazz. Blending together influences and ideas from various cultures can be a hotbed of innovation.

- **UNRELATED INGREDIENTS:** Whether you've caught your shirtsleeve on something and ripped it right before trying to make a first impression or realized a few miles into a hike that your toes were poking through your socks, we've all had a wardrobe malfunction at some inopportune time and wished for a magic repair. Fusing unlikely ingredients—bacteria and yeast—researchers at Penn State University have developed that magic wand, creating a biodegradable liquid that helps fabric bind to itself. When applied, the new substance self-repairs. Although the product is still in early development, the team is experimenting with a wide variety of mash-ups, including squid protein and exotic bacteria, to find fresh solutions for pesky problems.

- **CULTURAL DIVERSITY:** Israeli scientists are solving a humanitarian problem in Peru with a technique developed in ancient India. Borrowing the concept of *jugaad*, an ancient Hindi word meaning "a clever way to solve a problem using limited resources," researchers at Technion University (Israel's version of MIT) attacked the desperate clean-water supply problem in rural Peru. They developed a low-cost, easy-to-build machine that harvests moisture from the air and converts it into safe drinking water. The mash-up here was blending a diverse set of ideas, people, and approaches to solving a pressing issue in a novel way.

## THE MASH-UP: TRY IT OUT

Ready to explore the possibilities that associations could create for you? Time to set up your own mash-up lab!

1.  Make a list of products, services, and/or business models from those as different as possible from your industry.

2.  Now think about what you could take from these to mash up with your own products and services to offer something completely different. Play around with lots of combinations to discover your Reese's Peanut Butter Cup moment.

3.  Alternately, try to mash up two totally unrelated businesses and see what new and unique solutions you can come up with. Rather than thinking about your own business, mash-up two unrelated ones. How about a mash-up of a movie theater with a hospital? Cable TV with higher education? TikTok with life insurance?

If you're facing a problem or dealing with a setback, explore many different solutions that could be combined to create a new and more powerful approach. What can you create by mashing up with the learnings from the cruise industry? How about on-demand food delivery services? Maybe professional sports?

The mash-up is also effective at optimizing your internal processes. Think about what could be mashed up to improve performance, increase quality, or drive efficiency. What could you take from outside the current process and combine with existing efforts to create a new, better path forward?

# DIVERSITY IS A FORCE MULTIPLIER

Dump the vision of the singular tortured genius in the attic (or the C-suite). Let go of the midnight stroke of brilliance that cracks the code. Stop looking for your Medici-level patron. Pool knowledge, resources, and ideas, and be as open and excited about the possibilities, suggestions, and opportunities of others as you are about your own.

The mindset that two heads are better than one isn't new—creative problem-solvers just apply it more consistently, universally, and expansively. This is the core belief that bigger is better in nearly every aspect of the creative problem-solving process. A bigger market means not only more loot but more connections. A large quantity of ideas generally beats a single idea. More people with more diversity of thought bring more solutions, enthusiasm, and skills. Quantity, in all its forms, drives quality—especially when it comes to gathering the support and perspective that other people have to offer.

## START-UP SIMULATION

Pop quiz: What specific, key business components do cars, cigars, blood therapy supply chains, agricultural financing, professional athletics, and cosmetics share in common? What is the one obstacle they are all struggling with—the one that will make or break their models forever?

Answer? Well, if you came up with one, I think you should check your work.

Companies in each of these businesses have turned to Platypus Labs to help them with their unique obstacles—and the keyword there is *unique*. Having spent countless hours poring over the key business components, markets, and challenges they face, I can definitively assure you that there isn't a one-size-fits-all solution. Trying to shoehorn them into the six-step strategic framework approach that traditional consulting firms take is a relic from another era. The future of each of these companies depends on creative problem-solving—not a formula.

When clients hire Platypus Labs to help them solve a challenge, we don't come in with a prefabricated innovation framework; we leverage the mindset that diversity is a force multiplier. We carefully consider the specifics of the client and then handpick and assemble a diverse team of executives and experts in their respective fields, whether that is finance, technology, marketing, or something else. Then, we create an imaginary start-up to disrupt the company we are trying to help.

How does a team of start-up experts, unconstrained by the same limitations of our client, solve for the specific challenge at hand? Well, the answer is different each and every time—but the results are always incredible. By bringing in diversity of thought, we reinvent the client's challenge with new approaches, fresh thinking, and different perspectives. Because we curate a different team with a wide breadth of knowledge each time (rather than relying on the same MBAs using the same consulting models), the unique needs of the unique client we're working with stay at the forefront of the solution. This diversity of thought has allowed us to creatively problem-solve—we innovate the quest for innovation.

Creative problem-solvers are proudly efficient. We believe in working smarter, not harder—we want to achieve the maximum impact with the least amount of work. Let others do the work for you. Customers, fans, happy employees—they can be the most powerful form of endorsement or advertisement. Make sure you are utilizing them, authentically, to their full potential. By creating a structure that encourages others to contribute, you will be able to enjoy far bigger results than working alone. Borrow amazing ideas from your competitors, from other fields, from every source of inspiration you can access.

## Beliefs

- Many minds beat singular genius.

- Quantity drives quality.

- Big targets are easier to hit.

- One thousand paper cuts can create a deadly force.

## Characteristics

- Democratizes ideas

- Crowd- and open-sources innovation

- Embraces neural diversity

- Proudly efficient

## Tactics

- The imbizo group

- The borrowed idea

## TACTIC 7

# THE IMBIZO GROUP

At Platypus Labs, we often say that "expertise is the greatest enemy of innovation"—when we know (or think we know) too much about our industry, our systems and processes, or our customer, it's hard for us to adopt new methods and approaches. We must move far beyond the traditional hoarding of ideas and the "not invented here" mentality in order to meet today's challenges. Creative problem-solvers don't wait for one genius to have a light-bulb moment; they bring together people from diverse backgrounds, experience, departments, and even industries. Since innovation often occurs at the combustion point of opposing views, the more divergent ideas you can bring to a challenge, the better your results will likely be. Tapping into a wide set of ideas from a diverse pool of contributors is a powerful mechanism to stoke the flames of business innovation.

It's the power of the crowd, not the power of one, that holds real potential. The best brands know that innovation isn't bound by the walls of their own companies and that sometimes an experienced, engaged, or highly skilled crowd can crack the code for you. That's why crowdsourcing has become an integral part of modern business over the last twenty years; 90 percent of Fortune 500 companies employ some kind of crowdsourcing to gain different perspectives, increase brand awareness, and boost sales. With the advent of crowdsourcing software, it has become easier than ever for brands to crowdsource innovation, whether internally (from employees or stakeholders) or externally (brand fans, external experts, or the general public).

Creative problem-solvers see the gains that crowdsourcing has provided and take it to the next level by forming imbizo groups. *Imbizo* is the Zulu expression for gatherings of people from diverse backgrounds and disciplines who come together to discuss a challenge. Adopting this tradition within your creative process can provide a powerful tool for developing ideas and solving problems. Imbizo groups should be free-form, devoted to exploration, and have no specific targeted end goal. The key to success in these gatherings is to let go of the outcomes and simply allow the discussion to flow.

If your goal is to invent a new recipe for an award-winning bowl of chili, don't just enlist a small group of award-winning chili chefs. Go wide. Learn from vegetarians and chemists, senior citizens and tweens, chefs from international regions. Talk to people who have never tasted chili. If you're looking to truly innovate, tap into the power of the crowd. Who will you invite to participate in your imbizo group? What new perspectives do you hope to gain from them?

## THE IMBIZO GROUP IN ACTION

Whether you're working to save humanity or pursuing a more manageable endeavor, there is magic and inspiration in the crowd. These creative problem-solvers have explored the many ways imbizo groups can deliver value for their organizations, from fresh business models to marketing contests, to providing infrastructure, to designing their products and funding the cause.

## DRIVING THE JOKE

"Your move, BMW. The entirely new Audi A4."

The words adorned a large billboard in Los Angeles alongside a high-quality photo of the brand-new car. Clearly, the ad was rhetorical; the whole point was that there was no way BMW could possibly respond.

Except BMW is an innovative company. They know how to respond to a challenge with a nontraditional approach, how to adapt quickly. So within a week, directly in the sightline of the Audi billboard, BMW erected their own ad featuring an intimidating jet-black BMW 330i (the Audi A4's competition) with a giant, one-word headline: "Checkmate."

Two days later, Audi responded with another billboard. This ad featured a huge photo of the $145,000 Audi R8 supercar, highlighting its low profile, wide body, and gorgeous lines. The headline? "Your Pawn Is No Match for Our King."

The companies continued to furiously volley back and forth, trying to outdo each other with digital billboards, signs on actual cars driving through neighborhoods, and even a hot-air balloon showing the BMW Indy racing car touting the headline "Game Over."

Competitors like Lexus and Mercedes didn't enter the race; they sat silent on the sidelines, shut out of the conversation as BMW and Audi vied for the hearts and minds of customers.

In the end, Audi took the victory lap. The last few billboards that ran weren't even created by their ad agency—they were created by their customers. The innovators at Audi opened up the competition on social media and invited customers to submit ideas. Thousands flooded in, many of which were made into giant signs, including the headline "Chess? I'd Rather Be Driving."

Imagine engaging your customers so deeply that they fight to write your ads for you.

To me, the most inspiring part is the fluidity of this campaign. This was no strategic committee meeting with demographic data in a windowless room, crafting a scheme to get customers. There was no top-down mandate from the executive team. In fact, Audi cracked the code on their own failed marketing campaign. Their initial idea was to create an ad that BMW couldn't respond to; when BMW did, Audi engaged with a playfulness and a competitive spirit that was so much fun to watch that their customers couldn't wait to engage!

While BMW and Audi engaged their customers by getting them to write the ad copy, the leaders at global shipping company DHL couldn't afford to engage in a billboard war. While they had the best delivery times and reliability in many parts of the world, it was becoming increasingly difficult and expensive to communicate their competitive advantages. Rather than blowing millions for flashy ads, DHL took another path to creating an imbizo group. They prepped oversized packages for shipment in thermoactivated foil, which, cooled down below the freezing point, turned jet black—then called up their competitors to make the deliveries to highly visible locations across a busy European city.

As the temperatures rose, though, the specialized packaging revealed its secret. Each box turned bright yellow with bold red lettering that read "DHL IS FASTER." Competitors were toting around huge, bright billboards in DHL's corporate colors that alerted the public who was the best choice for shipping. Curious passersby reacted with giggles and sneers, all of which was caught on film by DHL's hidden cameras and released online. The video compilation has since been shared over forty million times—which means over forty million people now chuckle when they see a DHL logo and remember that "DHL IS FASTER."

Viral marketing has been around for ages, and word of mouth is the most effective sales approach for many organizations. To tap into this artery of opportunity, you must craft a win-win environment that rewards the person doing the sharing with social credibility. If the reward is there for the sender, the message will amplify.

## PROVIDE THE TOOLS

During the California gold rush in the mid-1800s, most wide-eyed miners ended up broke. Those who profited the most weren't those in search of gold but the ones who furnished the supplies. Motivated miners needed pickaxes, shovels, tents, provisions, and other tools of the trade.

Similarly, many businesses are now providing the modern-day equivalent of tools and supplies to facilitate imbizo groups. Transcriptic, a company based in the heart of Silicon Valley, offers biotech researchers access to "a fully automated cell and molecular biology laboratory, all from the comfort of your web browser." The company allows people from all over the world to submit ideas and experiments through a simple web interface; then the experiments are conducted inside an advanced laboratory environment. Transcriptic democratizes science by allowing people around the globe the opportunity to pursue their scientific curiosity without the traditional barriers of time, lab space, equipment, materials, or staff.

When you need a solid map to get from one place to another, surely you turn to the most obvious and trusted source: Rand McNally. Right?

From 1856 until the end of the twentieth century, Rand McNally was the leader in maps. The company had the best cartographers in the world and distributed everything from railroad maps and US river maps to city guides and road atlases. They had retail travel stores in twenty-nine major cities and were the first company to embrace a numbering system for US highways. The company was synonymous with maps and geography and was the go-to source for academics, consumers, and businesses alike.

When interactive maps such as MapQuest hit the scene, Rand McNally was still able to hold their ground. In fact, they were a leader in embracing technology, creating one of the first digital maps back in 1982. They were able to keep up with tech, but it was the crowd that left them in the dust. Despite their massive team of over four thousand people across four business groups, ultimately, they couldn't match the brainpower of the crowd.

Born over one hundred years later in a small town in Israel, a new mapping company took a different approach. Instead of the broadcast model of designing and selling maps from trained experts to the general public, Waze inverted the model. Their approach was to offer a free mapping platform in which consumers themselves became the source of value. As customers used the free mobile app, which offered basic functions such as road maps and driving directions, the insight from users became the inherent value. The map service becomes more powerful through the crowd of its users—the more people interact, the more value they create.

Users report information in an easy-to-use interface, which provides other users important insight. People update the map in real time, which offers things that Rand McNally could never provide; car accidents, traffic jams, and speed and police traps all pop up as an alert to the user, who can then select alternative routes. Waze also identifies the lowest-cost fueling options to a user along her route. Anonymous data, such as traffic speed and location, is gathered and sent back to the platform, allowing it to self-improve on a continuous basis. Waze leverages the power of the crowd to update their mapping solution continuously. The world-class cartographers at Rand McNally are no match for the now 130 million people using and updating Waze in real time.

The glaring contrast is also evident in each company's business performance. Rand McNally suffered through years of setbacks and layoffs. As the revenue dwindled, so did the workforce, which shrank from a peak of nearly five thousand people down to just three hundred today. The company was bought and sold, each time for a significant reduction in price, and succumbed to Chapter 11 bankruptcy. Waze, on the other hand, rose quickly against giant competitors such as Apple Maps, MapQuest, Facebook, and Google Maps. The company was purchased by Google in 2013, just seven years after its humble beginnings, for $1.1 billion.

Business models based on imbizo groups abound. Wikipedia upended *Encyclopedia Britannica*, World Book, and Microsoft's

*Encarta* by leveraging millions of people to author their content. UTest is a platform of over 35,000 professionals that offers software testing services for companies looking to take their quality to the next level. The value of Yelp, TripAdvisor, and Angie's List is derived from the collective wisdom of millions of people contributing opinions and insights, which in turn provides a more robust alternative to traditional review services such as Zagat's, Fodor's Travel Guides, and the Yellow Pages, respectively.

## DO US A FLAVOR

Your entire business need not be a community platform to benefit from the imbizo group. Take a traditional CPG company like Frito-Lay's namesake brand, Lay's Potato Chips. Though they are not in a position to crowdsource production, distribution, or real-time data, they've still been able to leverage the power of the imbizo group through a clever campaign called "Do Us a Flavor."

In 2012, the company announced a contest for new chip flavors. Thousands of ideas were submitted from loyal chip fans for the chance to win a big prize and bragging rights if their chip recipe became a hit. The campaign was such a success that the company now continues to build on the concept each year. The 2013 winner, cheesy garlic bread–flavored chips, contributed to an 8 percent sales increase in the three months after its release.

By 2015, things were really rolling. That year's challenge was to suggest flavors based on US cities; the winner would receive either $1 million or 1 percent of the flavor's net sales for the first year, whichever amount was higher. Tens of thousands of suggestions came from every corner of the US, including the Philly cheesesteak, Buffalo chicken wings, and Chicago deep-dish pizza. The contest raised awareness, captured media attention, and helped the brand stand out in a crowded category. Finalists Greektown gyro, West Coast truffle fries, and New York Reuben were eventually toppled in an online consumer vote, crowning southern biscuits and gravy as the 2015 winner. The ideas of the crowd, combined with providing an engaged sense of ownership to their customers, continues to drive delicious growth and profits for Lay's.

This creative problem-solving technique has already hit mainstream business. From electronics to air travel, you can see imbizo groups at work. Samsung, a company previously known for its "walled garden" mindset, recently debuted the Open Innovation Center in Palo Alto. The center entices entrepreneurs and innovators to collaborate with Samsung by offering capital, support, working space, and other rewards. Air New Zealand also took an imbizo group approach for the launch of its new 777-300 aircraft. Tapping their customers from around the world, Air New Zealand got ideas for cocktails, eye masks, seating configurations, food offerings, and even boarding processes. The influx of creativity allowed them to spice up their new plane, engage with customers, and set the bar for airlines like Emirates and Cathay Pacific, which quickly followed suit.

## COMMUNITY CURES

When Pete Frates, a former Boston College baseball player, was diagnosed with the degenerative condition amyotrophic lateral sclerosis (ALS, or Lou Gehrig's disease), he decided to try to raise money and awareness around the disease. Turned on to an unconventional challenge by a friend in the ALS community, he recorded himself dumping a bucket of ice water on his head to the dulcet tunes of "Ice, Ice, Baby," then sent the video off to friends—including some big names in the professional sports world—with a challenge: within twenty-four hours, dump a bucket of ice water on your own head and share the video to raise awareness, or, for a less frigid alternative, donate one hundred dollars to ALS research.

The Ice Bucket Challenge gained momentum, spreading through celebrities and social media like wildfire through the summer of 2014. By August 13, there were more than 1.2 million Ice Bucket videos on Facebook and nearly 10 million more on You-Tube. In addition to building unprecedented awareness, more than 739,000 new donors contributed nearly $115 million to the cause, which has helped fund research that has identified a contributing gene and developed new drug therapies. The Ice Bucket Challenge has now become a yearly tradition and is heralded as one of the most successful fundraising campaigns in history.

Frates died in 2019 at the age of thirty-four, but his creative problem-solving lives on. He did not invent the Ice Bucket Challenge; he was not in the lab researching genetic code. But his contribution in engaging the imbizo group is undeniable. Pete Frates did not create meaningful results alone—but by leveraging the power of others, he has changed the future for people living with this debilitating condition. Recognizing the fun potential of the experience, Frates drove international buzz and celebrity participation. Everyone's participation was highly rewarded via social media and through peer interactions, and each instance created many more. Millions of people participated or learned about the challenge and ultimately took action.

## BUYING LIFE WITH AN EMBRACE

Infant and maternal mortality is one of the largest problems facing the world today. Though women in developed countries are not immune to these dangers, women and children in developing countries are disproportionately at risk. According to the World Health Organization, in 2015, 4.5 million babies died within their first year of life; approximately 1 million of those die on the day of their birth. The worst part is that babies are dying from things that are preventable—the leading causes of death are complications relating to being born prematurely or at a low birth weight.

Babies born preterm or at very low birth weights lack the body fat to regulate their body temperatures. Traditional incubators are cost-prohibitive, and they require constant electricity and training that is not always feasible. In rural areas, the nearest incubator is often hours away and the journey too costly for mothers to afford.

During the Design for Extreme Affordability course as part of the Stanford MBA, Jane Chen and her team were tasked with designing something that could serve as a neonatal incubator—for less than $200 (or 1 percent of the cost for a traditional medical-grade incubator, which is about $20,000).

Chen and her classmates intentionally avoided looking into existing solutions and focused on the problem instead. Since 40 percent of premature births worldwide occur in India, they traveled there to get hands-on experience in impoverished areas where technology like this is needed most.

The team fell in love with the problem—these incredible mothers who would do anything to save their babies—and rapidly experimented many different possible materials, shapes, and details, until they refined their product into a viable solution. By the time they left their program, they had a revolutionary lifesaving technology and $125,000 in seed money to back the product.

The solution, the Embrace, looks nothing like an incubator at all but like a little cocoon. It is seamless and waterproof on the inside, which makes it easy to disinfect and reuse, and it has a removable packet of waxlike substance in the back, which can be heated with boiling water and maintains human body temperature consistently for up to eight hours before needing to be changed or reheated. The best part? The total cost for one Embrace is only twenty-five dollars.

The Embrace team had a product that fulfilled a real need, they had an unbelievably reasonable price point, and they had some capital, so what could go wrong?

Well, in the places that need Embrace the most, they had to rely upon local and national governments to pay for the devices and training. Unfortunately, this funding proved to be sporadic and unreliable. And in order to provide training, conduct clinical trials, and improve these distribution problems, they were going to need a much bigger and steadier source of income.

Jane and her team weren't going to give up on helping babies and mothers, so Jane got the idea to create an imbizo group that could drive the results that they needed. If parents in America could buy something for their own babies while supporting parents in impoverished areas of the world, not only would it help her team achieve their mission of saving as many babies as possible, but it would spread the word about the problem and get more people involved. So, Embrace stayed a nonprofit organization while Chen started a new company called Little Lotus.

Embrace owns the intellectual property to the technology and continues to spread the devices and training about caring for premature infants to areas in need. Little Lotus, a for-profit social enterprise, licenses the Embrace technology and sells it to hospitals and governments. The Little Lotus products are inspired by NASA fabric, which helps babies regulate their body temperatures, improving the length and quality of their sleep—a win-win for parents and babies. Using the one-to-one model, the proceeds from each Little Lotus product go to the distribution of an Embrace and the related training in the developing world. Parents in developed countries get quality products to help their little ones get more sleep while investing in the health and welfare of families around the world. The lives of over two hundred thousand babies have been saved through the Embrace technology. Instead of doing all the work herself, Jane found a way to leverage the resources of many people to advance her product and crack the code.

TOMS Shoes famously branded this one-to-one model where business meets philanthropy. For every pair of shoes purchased, the company donates a second pair to someone in need in a developing country. The "buy one, give one" model rocketed the company to tremendous instant success. When launching their e-commerce eyeglasses company, the founders of Warby Parker borrowed the model and offered the same "buy one, give one" approach. This model has since been replicated by dozens of other companies, who now offer "buy one, give one" dog food, baby clothes, cosmetics, books, and toothbrushes. It's a form of democratic funding that everyone gains from.

## NOT IMPOSSIBLE

Mick Ebeling was in Venice Beach, California, more than eight thousand miles away from the Nuba Mountains in war-torn South Sudan, but his heart still hurt as he read Daniel's *Time* interview: "If I could die today, I would, so I will not be a burden to my family." The boy had lost both his arms when bombs fell near his village, and he needed constant help for even the most basic tasks.

In 2009, Mick launched Not Impossible Labs, which takes on seemingly impossible missions and then uses creative problem-solving principles to conquer them, seeking to develop innovative solutions that can ultimately be replicated and scaled for the sake of improving humanity. They create imbizo groups to seek solutions from inventors, technologists, and dreamers around the globe.

Mick and his team at Not Impossible Labs met to discuss Daniel's plight and got working on the problem. They were able to create a solution using a 3D-printed prosthetic arm so he could feed himself, contribute to his community, and regain his dignity. They also leveraged their invention to help thousands of others in developing countries.

A jazz vocalist named Mandy Harvey was dealt an unimaginable setback at age eighteen when a rare disease attacked her ability to hear—putting her career and future in grave jeopardy. Within nine months, the disease took its toll: Mandy was completely deaf.

Somehow, she summoned the inner strength to continue her musical journey. Still possessing perfect pitch and timing, she decided to continue singing despite the fact she couldn't hear a single note. Mandy has been performing professionally for nearly a decade as the only completely deaf jazz singer in the world.

The creative problem-solvers at Not Impossible Labs set out to develop a way for Mandy to "hear" her music once again. Instead of working insulated within their organization, they went wide, issuing the challenge to the entire creative problem-solver community. They enlisted the ideas of scientists, research geeks, artists, and even computer hackers.

The answer emerged not as a single lightning bolt of inspiration but as a small concept that was built upon by many minds over time: since her auditory capacity could not be restored, what if they tapped into one of her other senses to allow her to embrace the music?

Their ingenious solution was put to the test in November 2015. Mandy was outfitted with a series of small motors that attached to various parts of her body (wrists, ankles, waist). The motors created small vibrations, triggered by computer sensors, that did the hearing for Mandy. They vibrated in different ways for different periods of time depending on a number of factors in the music, including tempo, pitch, and volume. For the first time in seven years, Mandy played with her band and "heard" the music in a rich, multisensory experience. Tears ran down her face as she connected with her music at a level inaccessible to her for nearly a decade.

Mick's unorthodox practices embody creative problem-solving at its finest: a burning curiosity and willingness to confront conventional wisdom, preferring democratized ideation from a diverse and vast array of contributors to single bets from entrenched "experts." Conducting low-cost, controlled, high-volume experiments. Finding a hole in the problem and then exploiting it to its logical end. Believing that no barrier is impenetrable.

When Mick first set out to cure some of the world's most vexing problems, he knew he couldn't do it alone—or even with a small team. There were already well-funded research labs taking on many of the same challenges in a traditional way, with solid equipment, detailed action plans, and lab-jacketed scientists toiling away in isolation.

Deciding that big problems needed a wider and more diverse set of answers, Mick built Not Impossible Labs on the foundation of the imbizo group, confident that with diversity of thought, culture, and experience, a group of dozens, hundreds, or thousands of people pecking away at a problem uncovers more compelling results. The Not Impossible team attacks some of humanity's greatest challenges by releasing the problems to the world rather than trying to solve them alone.

Imbizo groups are not for the faint of heart; they require a serious ego check. Ebeling explains that he actually seeks to *not* be the expert: "Surround yourself with people that make you feel stupid.

When you're the dumbest guy on the team, you know you're going to end up with a killer solution."

Now, taking on perhaps their most impossible challenge yet, the team is setting out to "hack water." They have created an imbizo group from a worldwide network of scientists, software engineers, artists, statisticians, architects, musicians, and philosophers. They are tapping into a robust community of creative problem-solvers who love to use their skills for something good. As ideas collide from a construction worker and an academic, mixed in with insight from a food chemist and a civil planner, completely new solutions emerge. As large problems go unsolved with insular approaches, Not Impossible Labs is forging new ground by leveraging the power of the crowd.

## THE IMBIZO GROUP: TRY IT OUT

1. The most important part of the imbizo group strategy to remember as you look to employ it to crack your own codes is the principle—diversity is a force multiplier. These exercises help you engage and collaborate with people, whether those people are your external customers or internal teams.

2. Identify an innovation challenge of your own and think how you can geometrically expand the source of ideas by leveraging the imbizo group. Could you create a contest to attract a wide range of ideas from as many people as possible? Could you tap into an existing community of people to secure a large and diverse set of ideas?

3. Look at your current problem-solving strategies, and give an honest assessment of where you stand on the closed-to-crowd continuum. If you're not yet comfortable seeking input from millions, how could you expand your imbizo group by 20 percent, 50 percent, or 80 percent to solicit a broader perspective?

4. In your business, have you built systems or infrastructure that you could sell to the crowd (your own version of pickaxes and shovels)? If you have a large sales team, perhaps you could allow others to access it to sell their goods and services to your customers while you take a piece of the action. Do you have a facility, equipment, or technology that sits dormant at times and could be resold to others?

5. What is the most important message you need to send to the world right now (marketing, investor relationships, media, etc.)? What are some ways you could use imbizo groups instead of traditional approaches? Brainstorm how nontraditional motivators, such as social standing, desire to share human experience, or the competitive spirit, can be harnessed in a responsible way to encourage others to spread the word on your behalf.

## TACTIC 8

# THE BORROWED IDEA

One of the greatest artists in history, Leonardo da Vinci, was also one of history's greatest inventors and earliest creative problem-solvers. He created detailed plans for inventions, that, at the time, had to seem nothing short of crazy. In the 1400s, when many people were scared that bathing would give them diseases, Leonardo was drawing out plans for armored chariots and a thirty-three-barrel machine gun. Today, one of his better-known concepts is a flying machine, which incorporated structural elements from birds and bats. His humanesque robot, of course, drew heavily from human anatomy to enable its movements.

They say imitation is the sincerest form of flattery, and borrowing is a crucial strategy for creative problem-solvers. Borrowing involves taking an idea, concept, or approach from a completely different realm and applying it to crack your code. You may gain inspiration from the arts, nature, other industries, or related problems.

The core concept is pattern recognition: finding inspiration from a completely different aspect of life, studying its essence, and then applying it in a novel way. After a pattern or concept is recognized, you can use it on your task at hand. Henry Ford's groundbreaking automotive assembly line was actually a concept borrowed from the meat-packing industry. With the recent success of on-demand ground transportation, a whole host of companies have emerged trying to become the Uber of health care, tailoring, accounting, and cold-pressed juices.

Too often we look for inspiration exclusively within our own industries, companies, or histories, then get frustrated when our ideas lack imagination. Borrowing ideas or inspiration from outside your industry or sphere of influence can drive innovation. Expand your perspective into completely different arenas to discover fresh possibilities. Look outside of your industry; look to nature; look anywhere totally unrelated. Find things that work really well somewhere else. Ask yourself why, and see if it could translate to your work. Ask yourself how someone else would solve your problem—a chemist, a textile artist, Neil deGrasse Tyson, Olivia Pope.

Borrowing can work in many directions. You may be stuck on how to motivate your customer service agents and then discover a fresh approach by learning how zookeepers manage herds of rhinos. (Metal-cutting company Valenite studied the jaw patterns of predatory fish clamping down on their prey in order to find innovative ways to beat their competition.) Borrowed ideas may even help you decide what to pursue next.

Too often we double down on existing practices when looking to advance our efforts. But as creativity expert Edward de Bono famously said, "You can't look in a new direction by looking harder in the same direction." Borrow new perspectives, and watch your world and business grow in crazy new directions.

# THE BORROWED IDEA IN ACTION

Borrowing from their competition, from closely related fields, from industries they admire, and from the natural world, the creative problem-solvers in these examples have innovated and invented new solutions to crack their codes.

## BLAZIN' FAST AND RIDING LOW

From Subway to SweetGreen, Chipotle to Chopt, the assembly-line restaurant has become the new staple to create inexpensive, quick, and customized meals, filling the gap between limited-option fast food and special-request restaurants. Some patrons choose to start with a menu staple and doctor it up, while others elect to start from scratch and build something of their own design—either way, you know you're walking out quickly with something tailored to your needs. This intersection has taken the food industry by storm, spreading beyond the sandwich or salad. It's safe to say that every type of cuisine could be adapted—except pizza.

When Rick and Elise Wetzel, the founders of Wetzel's Pretzels, looked for a similar concept in the world of pizza, they were struck by the obvious limitation that had stopped others before them from borrowing this concept for the pizza market. Pizza crusts need twelve to forty minutes of baking time; you can go NASCAR fast on every other element, but fast, customizable pizza crusts would take a time machine. Pizza was unadaptable to this model—it could either be fast and rigid, like the Little Caesar's five-dollar hot-and-ready pizza with no customization, or slow and personalized by ordering ahead or settling down in a restaurant while you waited for your specialty pie.

The Wetzels were so set on borrowing this business model for pizzas, however, that they just invented a time machine (every barrier can be penetrated, right?). The breakthrough, thin-crust pizzas baked in a special-built, extremely hot oven (900-plus degrees, 60,000 BTUs), now brings a customized masterpiece to life in only three minutes at over three hundred Blaze Pizza stores. By solving the seemingly insurmountable hang-up that had stumped other fast, customizable entrepreneurs, they've been able to borrow and adapt the most successful model in their wider industry.

## REMEMBER THE AEROCYCLE?

Since Henry Ford invented the assembly line in 1913, it has been borrowed by industry after industry to creatively solve challenges and free up more resources for innovation. Although Ignaz Schwinn, the grandfather of leisure bicycles, founded his company in 1891, he certainly borrowed the model to create his own eponymous empire. From his tiny rural German town, Schwinn studied the market conditions and saw demand taking off for two-wheelers. After a massive surge in which over a million units were produced by a multitude of competing bicycle manufacturers, by 1905, the industry was facing a huge slowdown. Everyone who wanted and could afford one of these new machines pretty much had one. Small shop after small shop went under, realizing they'd put themselves out of business.

Where everyone else saw an oversaturated market, Schwinn saw a clever opening. He began voraciously gobbling up limping competitors to build a modern factory that enabled him to mass produce low-cost bikes, opening up a much larger market. While this sounds obvious today, it was a bold and creative move in Schwinn's pre–World War I era.

This spirit of innovation continued to be a hallmark of Schwinn Bicycles for decades in all aspects of the business. Schwinn revolutionized all aspects of the bike, driving major breakthroughs in tires, seating, handlebars, gears, brakes, and design. They were at the innovative forefront of bicycle racing, manufacturing, retail and distribution, branding, and product design. They were anything but static. By the 1950s, Schwinn was the industry leader; they not only pioneered new products—they upended traditional distribution approaches. At the time, most bikes were sold to mass retailers and privately labeled (e.g., a Sears Supreme or a Woolworth's Racer). But Schwinn insisted their name and guarantee appear on all bikes. They sold to a vast network of distributors, ultimately letting the retailers capture far more profit per bike than possible with the entrenched model. Since retailers and distributors made more cash by selling Schwinn bikes than anything else, you can easily guess which ones they recommended most aggressively to customers.

Schwinn was a shining example of how a company can crack the code through borrowing. People didn't crave Schwinn bikes because of their outstanding business models or just for their quality—they wanted them because they were cool. In 1933, Ignaz's son, Frank W. Schwinn, introduced a radical new concept: a bike that looked like a motorcycle. The Aerocycle had chrome fenders, an imitation gas tank, a shiny headlight, and a push-button bell. Instead of milking the company's cash cow, F. W. and team pioneered uncharted territory. The Aerocycle, also known as the "cruiser" or "paperboy," quickly became the industry standard, driving the company to new heights of growth and profitability. Even during their later decline, a glimpse of hope shined through with Schwinn's invention of the Stingray, a bicycle design representing a low-rider motorcycle with a low-slung banana seat and raised handlebars. Borrowing on the design and cache of the motorcycle made many generations of Schwinns more than just any old bike.

## SIMPLE INK

We can find another amazing example of borrowing in the bicycle industry today. VanMoof isn't just *any* Dutch bicycle manufacturer. The rides they produce are the Tesla of commuter bikes—the highest of the high-end. These technological marvels are built to last a lifetime and hand assembled before they're shipped directly to your doorstep. When you're waiting for the large corrugated VanMoof box to arrive, you're waiting to step into the future of urban biking.

Except a lot of expectant VanMoof clients were finding the future much less than promised. The bikes were as amazing as promised—if they got there in one piece. Too many boxes arrived all beaten up, shredded by the shipping progress. VanMoof's unquestioning customer satisfaction policy was strained to breaking with the number of exchanges, refunds, and returns. It was not only expensive—it was damaging the brand's reputation.

So, the leaders got together and started ideating solutions. One person threw out, "We could double the packaging to protect the bikes." Another said, "We could hire a white-gloved courier service to hand-deliver and guarantee their safety."

Someone else muttered, "How the hell can the electronics industry ship their much more delicate flat-screen TVs directly to the doors of their customers with only a fraction of the damage?"

Long story short, VanMoof, borrowing from the electronic industry, started printing an image of a flat-screen TV on the outside of their boxes. The extra ink costs fractions of a penny more . . . but it has reduced the amount of breakage by over 75 percent overnight!

## SPRAY-ON SKIN

If the last twenty-five years were the era of IT transformation, it's been suggested that the next twenty-five will be health care's day in the sun. Due to major advances in biotech, stem cell research, nanotechnology, advanced drug therapy research, and wearable devices, the way we live and how we treat the sick is poised for massive transformation. And the source of many breakthroughs already underway is found in borrowing.

Serious burns are one of the most painful injuries humans endure; they often take months to heal and are treated by complex skin grafts, which are painful and prone to infection. They may never heal completely and often result in unsightly scars and years of complications. Dr. Jörg Gerlach, a German physician and researcher, has focused his life's work on skin cell treatments, transplants, and devices. He spent years helping patients recover from a variety of traumas, including severe burns.

Looking to advance his field and provide much-needed relief to patients, instead of looking for new ideas within the existing treatment options, Dr. Gerlach tapped into a most unlikely source of inspiration: spray paint. Observing how graffiti artists use spray cans to evenly dispense paint when tagging buildings in urban settings, Dr. Gerlach borrowed the concept and applied it to treating burns. His invention, the SkinGun, closely resembles an electronic spray gun and uses a mixture of saline solution and self-donated stem cells from a burn victim. The mist is evenly applied to a burn, allowing fresh layers of skin to regrow quickly. The process eliminates infection, reduces pain, and decreases the healing time of a serious burn from six or more agonizing months down to a couple of days. Plus, the end result is a far better outcome, often completely avoiding scarring.

Dr. Gerlach discovered a new and better idea by looking outside his field of study. In 2013, he was able to sell the SkinGun technology and related processes to RenovaCare, Inc., a company committed to worldwide distribution of this important medical device. Dr. Gerlach did well and did good by borrowing an idea from an unlikely and totally unrelated arena.

Like Dr. Gerlach, Amay Bandodkar spends a lot of time with skin. Instead of regrowth, Amay, along with a team of nanoengineers at the University of California, San Diego, is focused on using skin as a sensor to provide important medical information to both patients and healthcare professionals. Currently, most people with diabetes use small pinpricks to draw blood and then test the blood droplet with an expensive machine to monitor and control their glucose levels. This process often has to be repeated multiple times each day. Due to the discomfort, inconvenience, and costs, many patients forgo regular testing, resulting in serious and sometimes even fatal medical complications.

With the support of professor Joseph Wang's lab at the Nano-engineering Department and the Center for Wearable Sensors, Bandodkar borrowed a far better approach from a concept that may seem antithetical to health care: tattoos. What if a wearable, temporary tattoo could measure glucose levels through the fluid in between skin cells? Named by Mashable in 2015 as one of the twenty-six "Incredible Innovations that Improved the World," early prototypes have delivered encouraging results. The disposable tattoos are painless, easy to use for patients, and cost only a few cents per day—far less than traditional glucose testing systems. As development continues, the team hopes to integrate the tattoos with mobile devices, providing accurate, numerical readouts in real time. The system will also be able to monitor levels and send alerts to the patient, family members, or healthcare professionals.

## IT'S ONLY NATURAL

Across the pond, researchers in the Department of Informatic's Centre for Robotics Research (CoRe) at King's College, London, have borrowed another critical medical solution from an unlikely source. The team, focused on complex surgical procedures and the devices used to conduct them, were concerned with the limitations of modern macroscopic and robot-assisted surgical systems, which have difficulty maneuvering in confined spaces. The devices tend to be too stiff, potentially damaging internal organs or being unable to reach certain areas during a surgery, or they were too floppy, lacking the rigidity needed to conduct the procedures.

The team was inspired by the ability of an octopus's arm to quickly transform from stiff to floppy; at times, regions of the same arm could take on different levels of rigidity. This borrowed idea allowed the team to invent the STIFF FLOP (STIFFness controllable Flexible and Learnable manipulator for surgical OPerations). They essentially created a robotic version of an octopus's arm that can execute more precise, less risky surgical maneuvers.

Biomimicry—or human-made processes, devices, substances, or systems that imitate nature—is just a fancy term for borrowing ideas, patterns, or concepts from the wild. As this borrowing trend increases in popularity and efficacy, unlikely agents have joined forces to advance these studies and the innovations they contain: the San Diego Zoo launched a Center for Bioinspiration, helping corporate clients discover inspiration in nature, and academic institutions such as the University of Akron and Arizona State University now offer biomimicry programs for students and fee-based research for corporations.

Anthony Brennan, a professor of materials science and engineering at the University of Florida, was trying to figure out how to prevent barnacles from sticking to ship hulls. Instead of studying shipbuilding techniques or boat-coating materials, Brennan looked to nature. He observed that whales notoriously pick up large quantities of barnacles, but similarly sized sharks attract none. Further exploration of sharks led to the insight that microscopic textures on sharkskin ward off both barnacles and bacteria.

This insight led to the formation of his company, Sharklet Technologies, that recreates shark textures for a variety of surfaces. Today, business is booming as he protects medical devices, office desks, iPhone cases, and hospital countertops. "People are surprised that we found such an elegant, environmentally friendly solution from such a fierce predator," said CEO Mark Spiecker in an interview with *Inc.*

No matter where or how it is applied, borrowing ideas for products, services, and processes from other industries, nature, and the arts can be a powerful weapon in the innovation arsenal.

## THE BORROWED IDEA: TRY IT OUT

While a simple and effective concept, borrowing can take some practice to master even for the most adept creative problem-solver. As mentioned, expertise can often be the greatest enemy of innovation. Fresh eyes or a fresh perspective can be our biggest advantage, but in order to gain them, we need to step out of our traditional way of thinking to gain new insights and new possible solutions. The following exercises are some I've found incredibly effective while working with industry leaders and experts—if they can jump into other shoes, I'm sure you can too.

### EXERCISE: ROLESTORMING

1. Brainstorm a list of people who represent a wide range of indus-

tries or perspectives. Examples: an archaeologist, a four-year-old, someone living two hundred years in the future, Elon Musk, a Navy SEAL, a zoologist, Brad Pitt, Picasso, a professional bowling champion. The more diverse and strange, the better.

2. Take a stack of index cards, and write one name or role from your list on the back of each. Shuffle them up, and pass one to each participant.

3. Clearly articulate the challenge you're facing.

4. Begin brainstorming solutions—but not as yourself. Brainstorm as your assigned character. Think, move, and speak like them—and solve the problem as them (remember how Mr. Formal unleashed his creativity by taking on the persona of Ms. Piggy). Borrow the perspective and psyche of someone else, and invite them to your meeting so you can fully embrace how they might solve your problem and leave your own self, ego, and fear behind.

## EXERCISE: INVENT YOUR IDEAL ENEMY (A.K.A. "SLITHER")

Imagine that a brand-new, well-funded "ideal" competitor was just established—Slither—and they are coming directly after your business. Slither has no legacy issues and can proceed in any manner to win. They have access to capital, to smart people, and to great technology. Now imagine you were hired there to put your current company out of business. How would you, as a Slither team member, enhance your product or customer experience? How would you boost productivity, increase revenue, or drive operational efficiency? Name three things Slither is doing differently to put your company out of business. What strategies and tactics can you borrow and apply to your business?

## EXERCISE: WHAT MAKES YOU SO SPECIAL?

1. First, define the desired outcome of your challenge or opportunity. What would an ideal victory over it look like? What is the value that victory would bring? (Value doesn't have to be just economic—it could be social or emotional.)

2. Reviewing these elements, construct a "How might we . . . ?" question. "How might we . . . ?" opens the exploration space for new ideas and a range of possibilities, admits that we do not currently know the answer, and encourages a collaborative approach to solving it.

3. Next, identify four or more businesses that you'd like to borrow inspiration from to address your challenge and answer "How might we . . . ?" These businesses should ideally be from another industry, another country, etc. They should be from sources as disparate from your company and from one another as possible! Some of the more interesting companies

our team at Platypus Labs has enjoyed exploring and borrowing ideas from include the following:

**A.** Aleph Farms: 3D prints beef from tissues and cells

**B.** Algramo: sells bulk staples door-to-door

**C.** Baze: subscription services for personalized health supplements

**D.** Change Toothpaste: zero-waste toothpaste product

**E.** Sushi Singularity: uses biometrics to enhance the dining experience

**F.** Skyryse: the Uber of helicopter transportation

4. Write down all of the reasons that these businesses are special. It could be their customer experience, their pricing model, their distribution, their leverage of technology, their competitive advantage, or any other factor.

5. Use the inspiration from these businesses, and apply them to your challenge. Use the sparks to uncover new ways of going to business by starting your idea with "What if . . . ?"

On the next page, you'll find the Borrowed Idea worksheet we use at Platypus Labs:

# THE BORROWED IDEA WORKSHEET

| STEP 1 | STEP 2 | STEP 3 |
|---|---|---|
| Before you start ideating, extract insights and inspiration from various business models. You can go deep on a couple or look across many. | Use the inspiration to come up with new potential solutions for the challenge or opportunity you're working on.<br><br>Start your discussions with: "What If?" | Use the list of What If statements identified in Step 2 to come up with new and unique ways to solve for the challenge or opportunity at hand. |
| | | |

# CONNECTING IT ALL
# TOGETHER

Their spouses and families have no idea what they actually do while they're at work; very few people do. Their clandestine offices are hidden away from prying eyes, and access is screened through multiple ID checkpoints. Only this small group and the most senior management can get into their hidden lair.

But today, this group of diverse, creative problem-solvers is working on a key initiative outside the office. They've gathered at the swanky Hotel Trias in the town of Palamós, Spain. As the Mediterranean sun warms the gentle seaside breezes, a tall, unassuming man waits for everyone to get situated in one of the hotel's meeting rooms before beginning their briefing. He lays out the serious work ahead of them in the coming days before they assemble into tactical teams and get down to business.

So what is their business, exactly?

Toys.

That's right. The unassuming man at the front of the room is Erik Hansen, and the supersecret group he is briefing is Lego's FutureLab. They are on a weeklong getaway to bring together research, innovation, and play—to build the future of the company. Lego makes a physical product in an increasingly virtual world, so innovation is not a buzzword or fanciful experiment for the FutureLab; it's a matter of survival.

In 2003, Lego was nearly lost to the annals of toy history. The company was deferring to a purported expert with no toy experience who was arranging the corporate bricks from another country. They were reliant on licensing deals with major movies for surges in income, putting them at the mercy of film release schedules. And the previous Christmas season had left retailers in possession of too much of their Lego stock.

Experts said that Lego was facing obsolescence as video games and virtual worlds expanded. So, they were dumping all of their resources into digitally minded ventures that were out of sync with customer needs. Instead of approaching new products playfully, the company had quick, fear-based reactions. Trying to satisfy potential buyers who wanted less construction, they made kits with more molded pieces that required virtually no assembly. But the buyers they were trying to appease didn't really want to build at all; they wanted prebuilt toys. The builders that made up their base no longer recognized their once-beloved block-based toys.

Jørgen Vig Knudstorp took over in 2004 and steadied the Lego ship, helping Lego and FutureLab reach their full potential. But

FutureLab isn't the first time Lego embraced the innovator's mindset; it was already in their injection-molded plastic DNA.

Ole Kirk Christiansen set up shop in the little village of Billund, Denmark, as a carpenter in 1916. Christiansen's business shifted gears several times, from architecture to home goods, but when the Great Depression hit in the early 1930s, people had little interest in purchasing more of the ironing boards and ladders he'd been focusing on. So, Christiansen did a mash-up of his well-honed woodworking craft with something he thought would be easier to sell: toys. He began making small wooden toys and officially founded the Lego Toy Company in 1934.

About ten years later, Christiansen learned about injection-molded plastic. While talking with a supplier, he saw a selection of things that could be made with these machines. The item that captured his imagination was a small plastic brick, then being sold by a British company called Kiddicraft. He bought a machine, took a brick, and got to work.

Christiansen didn't just steal the Kiddicraft brick; he used the deconstruction tactic to take it apart and figure out how to make it work better. The result was a stud-and-tube design that could bind with other bricks strongly enough to withstand kids at play but still come apart easily. The result is what Lego calls "clutch factor." (It's what makes that satisfying popping noise when you attach and detach the bricks.)

Christiansen's process is now frequently repeated by the FutureLab. During their weeklong annual retreats, the highlight is the twenty-four-hour hackathon, when the teams use rapid experimentation to quickly test and cycle through ideas.

Lego doesn't just make colorful bricks, pirate ships, and teeny-tiny Harry Potters—they're also a research hub. Through independent research and partnerships with major universities and institutions, Lego creates their own imbizo groups to gain information about play from their customers: kids. Equipped with data about how kids think and play, the FutureLab comes to the hackathon ready to create. One such creation was Lego Fusion, a mash-up that allowed kids to integrate physical and digital realities.

Gathering insights and ideas directly from their customers has become a major boon for them in recent years, but years ago, Lego almost shut off this valuable pipeline of ideas. In 1998, attempting to fend off extinction by electronics, Lego partnered with MIT to release Mindstorms, a computerized yellow brick module that allowed kids to turn their Lego bricks into rudimentary robots.

Though we're probably still a few years away from the robot takeover, Mindstorms did take on a life of their own. Designed like all Lego products for kids, the company was shocked to learn that roughly half of all sales were to adults, for adults. A Lego fan at Stanford hacked the code in the Mindstorms module and began writing new code for it; within three months, over one thousand hackers were creating codes for Mindstorms robots.

Lego's initial response was defensive—their product had been violated and was being misused—and they called in senior management and legal teams to decide how to deal with the situation. As senior director of community engagement & events Tormond Askildsen explains, the company had two available reactions: they could either be "aggressive, protective, controlling," or they could say, "Wow . . . this is interesting." The traditional model is to circle the wagons and draw up the lawsuits, but creative problem-solvers explore, question, and experiment. Lego chose compasses over maps, and Mindstorms are still in production today.

This opened Lego up to the power of imbizo groups, which led them to execute a major judo flip in 2007. When Chicago-based architect Adam Reed Tucker lost his job, he channeled his frustration in an unexpected way: he began to carefully construct landmark buildings entirely out of Lego. Tucker reached out to Lego executive Paal Smith-Meyer about the potential for adult Lego kits. Smith-Meyer was intrigued but knew he needed to take more to management before they would sanction breaking their business model. He sent Tucker the bricks to see what he could come up with. Tucker started at the end to create two hundred kits in his home, complete with instructions, box art, and packaging. Now, convinced that the project had potential, Lego took a gamble and did something previously unthinkable, releasing a line of their toys just for adults—the first of the architecture series. It not only sold well—it did so at twice the price point of the kids' kits.

Lego, in fact, embraces each of the core mindsets of the creative problem-solver.

- **EVERY BARRIER CAN BE PENETRATED**: From children to adult markets, from the physical to virtual worlds, from boys to girls, scientists to Harry Potter enthusiasts, and everything in between, Lego has created products that appeal to people across many demographics. Arguably, the biggest hurdle to reaching people around the world is language, but Lego created a product that transcends even this greatest of communication barriers.

- **COMPASSES OVER MAPS:** By not tying themselves to a map, Lego has been able to make unexpected detours, like veering away from their primary children's toy market to delighting adults with the Architecture series. But this mindset isn't just about going in new directions; it's about being able to retrace your steps when something has gone amiss and then course-correct. With some of their digital projects and overly molded, mostly assembled products, Lego saw that they didn't like the lay of the land and chose a new direction.

- **NOTHING IS STATIC:** Ole Kirk Christiansen knew this from the start—from wooden furniture to wooden toys to plastic toys, through three separate factories burning down, from the Kiddicraft brick to the Lego stud and tube, Christiansen was always willing to shake things up. The company has never stopped challenging itself and its users to imagine what may be possible and has added countless shapes, figures, accessories, and other plastic pieces throughout the years.

- **DIVERSITY IS A FORCE MULTIPLIER:** Even though the FutureLab work is top-secret, this R&D team is a collaborative effort. The activities on their annual retreat are team oriented and show just how important it is to pool a wide range of inputs. And after Mindstorms, Lego embraced the potential of collaboration outside the company, particularly with their customers. One such effort is their Japan-based Cuusoo project, which allows users to submit their dream Lego kits to a website for consideration. Those that get over ten thousand user likes are considered for the annual special-edition Cuusoo kit. The competition to become the next Cuusoo kit is just as popular as the kits themselves. As Lego's Tormod Askildsen brilliantly puts it, "We need to be aware that 99.99 percent of the smartest people in the world don't work for us."

The creative problem-solving at the heart of Lego has trickled down to its millions of users. Today, Lego embraces that some of their most avid and enthusiastic users are adults. And many Lego fans are tapping into their inner children to use Lego for very grown-up projects, from fully functional cars to livable houses, from recreating ancient Greek technology to public and private art installations.

Architects use Lego to mock up building plans; researchers at MIT use scale Lego cities to explore city-planning efforts. Studies out of the Yale School in New Jersey have even shown that Lego-based therapy can improve social outcomes for autistic children. One of NASA's California offices has a room filled with Lego bricks, where they dream up space missions and spacecraft; the *Juno* mission to Jupiter included specialized space-grade aluminum Lego mini figurines mounted to the outside of the craft.

Lego has released blockbuster movies of their own and no longer relies on licensing deals to hit their margins. They have responded to the needs of the changing world, creating highly anticipated kits for COVID-homebound adults and children alike and donating copious creative and educational resources for children impacted by school shutdowns. By embracing the innovator's mindset in their overall operations with a dedicated group of high-intensity creative problem-solvers, Lego has cracked the code. They've not only defined the childhood of millions, they're also defining the future of toys.

## YOU CAN CRACK THE CODE

Creative problem-solvers are the most valuable and coveted resources for any business, market, team, and community. As our worlds and challenges continue to expand, creative problem-solvers crack the codes and turn challenges into opportunities.

Creative problem-solvers aren't born—they're made. Becoming a creative problem-solver is a decision; even the most innately creative person in the world must decide to refine their innovative talents to produce remarkable results. Through this book, you've explored the mindsets and tactics that will allow you to harness this incredible force, and you can apply this information to systemically crack any code. If you're still not sure you're a creative problem-solver, start small—apply the tactics, and build the muscle. Once you've cracked your first code, take another hard look at the mindsets, and recognize how you've adopted them as your own.

The beauty of being a creative problem-solver (besides the astounding barriers you'll break, the innovations you'll achieve, and the progress you'll make—you know, the little stuff) is that you're always becoming more, growing your skills, and exponentially increasing your potential. Once you decide that you're a creative problem-solver—that every barrier can be penetrated, that you'll grab a compass rather than a map, that nothing is static, and that diversity is a force multiplier—you'll not only be able to use the tactics that support each of these mindsets to their greatest effect, you'll start to see areas in which they can be added to, expanded, and innovated. If you're itching for more tactics, come check us out at www.platypuslabs.com—I'm coming up with and hunting down new ones every day with my team at Platypus Labs, and we're always looking for more creative problem-solvers to test them out and make them better. Of course, when you start improving and inventing tactics of your own, please reach out to us at innovate@ platypuslabs.com—we can't wait to hear what you develop!

I hope you enjoyed the mindsets and tactics we covered in this book. I wish you all the success as you continue on your journey to become a creative problem-solver and crack the code!

# QUICK REFERENCE GUIDE

## THE MINDSETS

**EVERY BARRIER CAN BE PENETRATED**: Approach every problem, every step of a system, every obstacle with the understanding that it can be overcome; the question is not *if* but *how*. But assuming a problem can be solved is where the assumptions end. To triumph over barriers, the most successful creative problem-solvers assume nothing and take nothing at face value. When approaching any task or problem, proceed as if everything is up for debate—no information is set in stone, no system is infallible, no solution is fixed, no problem is ever permanently solved.

**COMPASSES OVER MAPS**: Creative problem-solvers have a general idea of where they're headed, but they go off into uncharted territory and maybe draw up a map later. This mindset is about curiosity and exploration. Using a map is perfunctory; it presupposes both the destination and the best way of getting there. Using a compass admits a general direction but surrenders playfully to the realities of the landscape, allowing the traveler to adjust course based on the lay of the land. A mountain is an opportunity, not an obstacle. Fall in love with the problem, not the solution, and constantly renavigate the problem based on the current landscape, rather than carefully retracing the mapped-out routes of previous solutions.

**NOTHING IS STATIC:** This mindset isn't about fearmongering but maintaining a constant thirst for knowledge and self-improvement. Creative problem-solvers are committed to constantly expanding and updating their skills and knowledge base. Complacency is simply not an option. Embrace, don't fear, change. Instead of waiting for someone else to corner you into change, constantly initiate it; actively court and choose change instead of running from it. From systems to solutions, nothing lasts forever, so relish learning, growing, and exploring new possibilities.

**DIVERSITY IS A FORCE MULTIPLIER:** Do away with the romantic notion of the singular genius in the attic (or the C-suite) in favor of diverse and democratized ideation. Pool knowledge, resources, and ideas—the more inputs, the better—and be as open and excited about the ideas of others as about your own. Expertise may be found in the unlikeliest of places. This mindset isn't new, but the best creative problem-solvers apply it more consistently and universally to crack the code.

# THE 8 KEYS TO UNLOCK INNOVATION

**DECONSTRUCTION:** If something isn't working or you're sure it could do better, take it apart. Break it into its smallest elements, seeing how the parts work together. Then put it back together—but differently. Add, subtract, or substitute elements for improved variations.

**RAPID EXPERIMENTATION:** Try lots of solutions to narrow down the best options quickly. This is about using a battering ram (or three), not picking a lock. Here, it's all about speed—attack a problem hard, intensely, even completely, in a short span of time.

**START SMALL:** How do you climb a mountain? One step at a time. Focus on a small win and then leverage that to create bigger, longer-lasting wins. Think of your problem as a wall—look for the tiniest hole, figure out how you can wiggle through, and then expand the hole until the whole wall is gone.

**START AT THE END:** Don't get hung up on your favorite solution. Start with knowing your ideal outcome, in vivid detail, and then work backward to imagine a new path to your perfect solution. If you want to do something that's never been done, you probably need to go about it in a new way, too, so start at the finish line.

**THE JUDO FLIP:** How should you solve a problem? Do the opposite. Whether it's flipping your first inclination upside down or following the opposite of what you're supposed to do, thumb your nose at expectations, and dare to do things totally differently.

**THE MASH-UP:** Sometimes the best solution isn't a new one but existing solutions combined and reimagined. Maybe you combine two strategies into one; maybe you take one of your strategies and combine it with something from another industry. The result is one elegant solution you can't imagine having lived without.

**THE IMBIZO GROUP:** Stop waiting for one genius to have a light-bulb moment. Bring together people from diverse backgrounds, experiences, departments, even industries. Two heads are better than one, three are better than two . . . you get the idea.

**THE BORROWED IDEA:** Stop looking in the usual places for solutions and inspiration. Look outside of your industry, look to nature, look anywhere totally unrelated. Find things that work really well somewhere else, and ask yourself why and if it could translate to your work. Pretend to be someone else, and approach your problem from a fresh and different perspective.

# 10 COMMANDMENTS OF BRAINSTORMING

Brainstorming is big at most organizations today, but in becoming ubiquitous, it has lost something. The invitation "Let's brainstorm about that" typically leads to a gathering in a conference room where the convener asks for ideas and then shoots them down as fast as they come up. Brainstorming has been compressed and made more efficient—killing its real purpose in the process.

The whole point of brainstorming is to let creativity shine. You need to be very careful not to let criticism stifle that creativity. The creative process must be supported, nurtured, and embraced wholeheartedly to generate good results. To that end, we've developed the 10 commandments of brainstorming, universal rules to help establish a framework for imagination and creativity.

Print out a copy of these rules and tape them to the wall before any brainstorming session. We'd also suggest you bring a bell, kazoo, drum, or other noisemaker to the session. Every time someone breaks one of the commandments, ring the bell or beat the drum. Make your whole team responsible for enforcing the rules and holding everyone else accountable. Think of the rules as non-negotiable and make sure everyone on your team agrees to them before any idea generation begins.

1. **THOU SHALT NOT JUDGE.** As ideas begin to flow, you must do everything in your power to let them flow. No one should be allowed to offer any judgment of any idea. The idea-generation phase is about generating ideas, not ranking them. Just let them run like the mighty Amazon. There will be plenty of time to evaluate them later.

2. **THOU SHALT NOT COMMENT.** Even if the person next to you throws out the stupidest idea you've ever heard, let the process continue. The slightest comment or criticism will change the mood in the room, and the group will start to clam up. The objective is to bring ideas to the surface, not to discuss them. The only acceptable comment is a very short "wow," "cool," or "sweeeeeet."

3. **THOU SHALT NOT EDIT.** Don't let your inner editor join the session. When you're brainstorming, it doesn't matter where the comma goes in the sentence or how best to word something. The font choice, color palette, and idea name are irrelevant. Editing is a left-brain activity that is completely

separate from idea generation. Keep it that way. First, let the ideas come out sloppy and uninhibited. You'll have plenty of opportunity to edit later.

4. **THOU SHALT NOT EXECUTE:** The second an idea hits the whiteboard, you can easily become distracted by thinking about execution. You'll wonder how the idea would come to life. What would it cost? Who would run it? What would the project plan look like? What would the financial implications be? Where would the work take place? When would we begin?

   Those are great questions for later, but avoid them at this stage. They are your left-brain in all its glory sneaking in and vying for a seat at the table. As important as that kind of thinking may be, it will quickly crush your creativity. Keep it out of the room.

5. **THOU SHALT NOT WORRY.** Fear is the single biggest blocker of creativity. It is pounded into us from childhood on. We learn in school that there is always one right answer and that mistakes should be avoided at all cost. You need to release that fear to unshackle your true creative potential. If you're leading the group, emphasize this before you begin. Tell your colleagues that every idea matters and that the whole point of the exercise is to get a lot of ideas on the board. To best create an environment where everyone feels comfortable taking risks and has no fear of embarrassment or negative consequences, set an example.

If you as a leader aren't afraid to toss out silly, outrageous ideas, you will enable others to release their fears as well, so that their most creative thinking can emerge.

6. **THOU SHALT NOT LOOK BACKWARD.** We can always learn a lot from the past, but it can also limit our ability to invent the future. Holding back an idea because we tried it once before and it didn't work out so well is highly limiting. Think how much the world changes every day. An idea today comes into a world with an entirely new set of circumstances, market conditions, technologies, and customer tastes. If it didn't work in the past, it may just have been ahead of its time. Or perhaps that idea, when revisited, will lead to a revised version that can carry the day.

Every idea is new at this moment, so share every single one that you believe has merit.

7. **THOU SHALT NOT LOSE FOCUS.** Idea sessions can easily dissolve into wandering and woolgathering. Don't let it happen. An idea might remind someone of a story she just has to tell. Or it might lead to taking on a different creative challenge or discussing a completely different topic. A right-brain creative state is so rare and so refreshing that its energy and excitement can cause a team to stray.

To solve this, keep what we call a parking lot list. When unrelated topics come up, put them on the parking lot list to be discussed another time. This will keep the group focused on the task at hand while still making sure that important concepts are remembered and can get attention later.

8. **THOU SHALT NOT SAP ENERGY.** There are two kinds of people: zappers and sappers. When you're with a zapper, you feel energized. You become engaged, you lean forward, and you feel stimulated, which is ideal for creative expression. Sappers are the folks who drain your energy. Even if you've just had six shots of espresso and four Red Bulls, you want to fall asleep after speaking with them for five minutes. Just as you manage the clock or manage a budget, manage energy.

   The collective energy of the room can build into a frenzy, unleashing brilliant ideas while everyone has a great time, or it can devolve into yet another boring, iPhone-checking, clock-watching drone session. Do everything you can to keep the energy up. High-fives, cheers, and positive vibes for all. Don't allow negativity and energy-draining commentary to suck the life from the room.

9. **THOU SHALT NOT COMPARE.** Comparing ideas is an insidious form of criticism that needs to be checked at the door with all other left-brain habits. Comparing usually contains an implicit criticism. "That's like the idea Jim had back in 2018" sounds harmless enough on the face of it, but think again. Remember Jim? Everyone hated him.

**10. THOU SHALT NOT MAKE FUNNY AT OTHERS' EXPENSE.**
Brainstorming can become quite jolly, and the temptation to start joking about what comes up can be hard to resist. But resist it you must. Laughter at the expense of an idea is a fast way to kill it.

Assiduously follow these commandments to prevent your brainstorming sessions from wasting everyone's time and producing only the three safe, same—and probably useless—ideas the group had last time. Brainstorming is a profoundly useful creative technique, but only if you use it properly.

# REFERENCES

## MINDSET 1

Nuñez, Michael. "Pablos Holman Wants You to Break Your Gadgets." *Popular Science.* 9 Mar. 2015. www.popsci.com/pablos-holman-wants-you-break-your-gadgets.

Soderbergh, Steven. *Ocean's Eleven.* 2001. Film.

"A Rich History." *Rust-Oleum Europe.* www.rust-oleum.eu/history.

Rethford, Wayne. "Robert Fergusson and Rust-Oleum Paint." *Scots Great and Small, People and Places.* www.chicagoscots.blogspot.com/2010/01/robert-fergusson-and-rust-oleum-paint.html.

"The History of American Graffiti:' From Subway Car to Gallery." PBS *NewsHour*. 31 Mar. 2011.www.pbs.org/newshour/art/the-history-of-american-graffiti-from-subway-car-to-gallery/.

Platypus Labs. Interview with Chad Price. Sept. 2020.

## MINDSET 2

Maeterlinck, Maurice. *The Life of the Bee*. New York: Dover Publications, 2006.

Reeves, Martin and Johann Harnoss. "Don't Let Your Company Get Trapped by Success." *Harvard Business Review*. 19 Nov. 2015.

Soffel, Jenny. "These RoboBees Could Pollinate Crops and Save Disaster Victims." *World Economic Forum*. 27 Jun. 2016. www.weforum.org/agenda/2016/06/the-bees-of-the-future-that-can-pollinate-and-save-disaster-victims/.

"Berkshire Hathaway." *Wikipedia*. 30 Sept. 2020. *Wikipedia*. Web.

"IBM." *Wikipedia*. 29 Sept. 2020. *Wikipedia*. Web.

"Pixar." *Wikipedia*. 25 Sept. 2020. *Wikipedia*. Web.

"Suzuki." *Wikipedia*. 17 Sept. 2020. *Wikipedia*. Web.

Connor, Deni. "Five Things You Don't Know about EMC" *Computer-World*. 5 Jul. 2007. www.computerworld.com/article/2542376/ data-center/five-things-you-don-t-know-about-emc.html.

Rouse, Margaret. "What Is Brute Force Cracking?" *Tech Target*. N.d. www.searchsecurity.techtarget.com/definition/brute-force-cracking.

Covey, Stephen R. *The 7 Habits of Highly Effective People: Powerful Lessons in Personal Change*. Revised edition. New York: Free Press, 2004.

Dryden, John. *Absalom and Achitophel*. Kessinger Publishing, 2010.

Ruddick, Graham. "How Zara Became the World's Biggest Fashion Retailer." 20 Oct. 2014. www.telegraph.co.uk.

Ferdows, Kasra, et al. "Zara's Secret for Fast Fashion." *Harvard Business School*. 21 Feb. 2005. hbswk.hbs.edu/archive/4652.html.

"The Complete History of Instagram." *We Are Social Media*. N.d. www.wersm.com/the-complete-history-of-instagram/.

"The Rise, Dominance, and Epic Fall—a Brief Look at Nokia's History." *GSMArena*. 12 Aug. 2015. www.gsmarena.com/ the_rise_dominance_and_epic_fall_a_brief_look_at_nokias_ history-blog-13460.php.

Loeb, Walter. "Zara's Secret to Success: The New Science Of Retailing." *Forbes*. 14 Oct. 2013. www.forbes.com/sites/walterloeb/2013/10/14/zaras-secret-to-success-the-new-science-of-retailing-a-must-read/#1da88b1e1332.

Fishman, Charles. "The Road to Resilience: How Unscientific Innovation Saved Marlin Steel." *Fast Company*. 17 Jun. 2013. www.fastcompany.com/3012591/marlin-steel-metal-baskets.

"Bose Corporation." *Wikipedia*. 21 Sept. 2020.

Porges, Seth. "Dr. Bose Tells All: Company Secrets, Why They Don't Publish Specs, and More." *TechCrunch*. 19 Sept. 2007. www.techcrunch.com/2007/09/19/dr-bose-tells-all-company-sercrets-why-they-dont-publish-specs-and-more/.

"The First 50 Years of Bose." *The Complete History and Future of Bose*. 30 Sept. 2016. www.dreamandreach.bose.com/en_US.

Scott, Bartie. "How Hillary Hooch and Trump Tonic Are Saving This 112-Year-Old Soda Business." *Inc*. 20 Jul. 2016. www.inc.com/bartie-scott/averys-beverages-trump-tonic-hillary-hooch.html.

"About." *Sorry as a Service*. 30 Sept. 2020. www.sorryasaservice.com/.

Odineca, Marija. "Sorry as a Service Admitted to TechStars London." *ArcticStartup*. 8 Jul. 2015. www.arcticstartup.com/article/sorry-as-a-service-admitted-to-techstars-london.

Platypus Labs. Interview with Martin McGloin. 20 Sept. 2016.

"Duke 101." *National Review*. 2 Nov. 2013. www.nationalreview.com/ article/362692/duke-101-interview.

Hoshaw, Lindsey. "Silicon Valley's Bloody Plant Burger Smells, Tastes and Sizzles Like Meat." *NPR.org*. 21 Jun. 2016. www. npr.org/sections/thesalt/2016/06/21/482322571/silicon-valley-s-bloody-plant-burger-smells-tastes-and-sizzles-like-meat.

"Impossible Foods." *Impossible Foods*. N.d. 30 Sept. 2016. www. impossiblefoods.com/.

Soller, Kurt. "The Impossible Burger Is Ready for Its (Meatless) Close-Up." *Wall Street Journal*. 14 Jun 2016. www.wsj.com/ articles/the-impossible-burger-is-ready-for-its-meatless-close-up-1465912323.

Green, Dennis. "The Real Story behind the Detroit-Made Watch Obama Just Gave to David Cameron." *Business Insider*. 17 May 2016. www.businessinsider.com/the-real-story-behind-shino-la-detroit-2016-5.

Linkner, Josh. Interview with Jacques Panis. 21 Apr. 2016.

## MINDSET 3

"Reese's Peanut Butter Cups." *Wikipedia*. 26 Sept. 2020.

"About Us." *Carvana*. 30 Sept. 2020. www.carvana.com/about-us.

Henry, Jim. "Carvana Used-Car Vending Machine Is Tip of the Disruption Iceberg." *Forbes*. 29 Nov. 2015. www.forbes.com/sites/jimhenry/2015/11/29/carvana-used-car-vending-machine-is-the-tip-of-the-disruption-iceberg/#2c69710d9f80.

"This Startup Raised $160 Million for Its 'Car Vending Machines." *Fortune*. 10 Aug. 2016. www.fortune.com/2016/08/10/carvana-car-marketplace-160-million/.

"AutoNation." *Fortune*. 30 Sept. 2016. www.beta.fortune.com/fortune500/autonation-136.

Alessi, Christopher. "Thyssenkrupp Reimagines the Elevator as a Hyper-loop for Buildings." *Wall Street Journal*. 19 Jul. 2016. www.wsj.com/articles/thyssenkrupp-reimagines-the-elevator-as-a-hyperloop-for-buildings-1468875762.

"History of Patagonia—a Company Created by Yvon Chouinard." 30 Sept. 2016. www.patagonia.com/company-history.html.

Adams, Susan. "How Prezi's Peter Arvai Plans to Beat PowerPoint." *Forbes*. 7 Jun. 2016. www.forbes.com/sites/forbestreptalks/2016/06/07/how-prezis-peter-arvai-plans-to-beat-powerpoint/#3ea4ba176bdd.

Curda, Pavel. "Prezi: Building a Successful Startup from a Small Country." *The Next Web*. 27 Jun. 2014. www.thenextweb.com/insider/2014/06/27/how-build-globally-successful-start-up-small-country/.

Linkner, Josh. Interview with Peter Arvai and Adam Somlai-Fischer. 11 Aug. 2016.

Burns, Mark J. "How Topgolf Flipped the Traditional Driving Range Model and Created a New Category of Entertainment." *Forbes*. 2 Mar. 2015. www.forbes.com/sites/markjburns/2015/03/02/how-topgolf-flipped-the-traditional-driving-range-model-and-created-a-new-category-of-entertainment/5caa94e5fbbc.

Carr, Austin. "Deep inside Taco Bell's Doritos Locos Taco." *Fast Company*. 1 May 2013. www.fastcompany.com/3008346/deep-inside-taco-bells-doritos-locos-taco.

Kavilanz, Parija. "This Liquid Could Let Torn Clothes Repair Themselves." *CNN*. 10 Aug. 2016. www.money.cnn.com/2016/08/10/technology/self-repairing-fabric/.

Messer, A'ndrea Elyse. "Self-Healing Textiles Not Only Repair Themselves, but Can Neutralize Chemicals." *Penn State University*. 25 Jul. 2016.www.news.psu.edu/story/418507/2016/07/25/research/self-healing-textiles-not-only-repair-themselves-can-neutralize.

"Ultimate Fighting Championship." *Wikipedia*. 30 Sept. 2020.

Weisul, Kimberly. "How This Startup Is Taking the Frustration Out of Multiple Medications." *Inc.* 24 May 2016. www.inc.com/kimberly-weisul/2016-30-under-30-pillpack.html.

# MINDSET 4

"Reese's Commercial." *The Hershey Company*. 1981.

"Temporary Tattoo Offers Needle-Free Way to Monitor Glucose Levels." *UC San Diego*. 14 Jan. 2015.www.ucsdnews.ucsd.edu/pressrelease/temporary_tattoo_offers_needle_free_way_to_monitor_glucose_levels.

"About Us." *Little Lotus*. 30 Sept. 2016. www.littlelotusbaby.com/pages/about-us.

Chen, Jane. "A Warm Embrace That Saves Lives." *TED Talk*. Nov. 2009. www.ted.com/talks/jane_chen_a_warm_embrace_that_saves_lives?language=en.

# REFERENCES

"Embrace." *Stanford University*. 2007. www.extreme.stanford.edu/
projects/embrace.

"Embrace Warmer | Infant Warmer." *Embrace Global*. 30 Sept. 2020.
www.embraceglobal.org/embrace-warmer/.

Restauri, Denise. "A Personal Story: How Low Cost Technology Is
Saving Babies' Lives." *Forbes*. 18 Nov. 2014. www.forbes.com/
sites/denis-erestauri/2014/11/18/a-personal-story-how-low-cost-
technology-is-saving-babies-lives/#43e14d997dc5.

Routson, Joyce. "Embracing a Way to Change the World." *Stanford
Graduate School of Business*. 1 May 2011. www.gsb.stanford.edu/
in-sights/embracing-way-change-world.

Maverick: *The Success Story behind the World's Most Unusual Work-place*.
Reprint edition. New York, NY: Grand Central Publishing, 1995.

Shaughnessy, Dan. "The Amazing Pete Frates Story Continues to
Inspire." *The Boston Globe*. 3 Mar. 2015. www.bostonglobe.com/
sports/2015/03/03/the-amazing-pete-frates-story-continues-in-
spire/vdfnJSntd5WjcxdurvsizL/story.html.

"The Incredible History of the ALS Ice Bucket Challenge!" ALS
Association. N.d. www.alsa.org/fight-als/edau/ibc-history.html.

"WHO | Infant Mortality." WHO. 30 Sept. 2016.www.who.int/gho/
child_health/mortality/neonatal_infant_text/en/.

Yakowicz, Will. "This Space-Age Blanket Startup Has Helped Save 200,000 Babies (and Counting)." *Inc.* 27 Apr. 2016. www.inc.com/magazine/201605/will-yakowicz/embrace-premature-baby-blanket.html.

Fawzy, Farida. "Ice Bucket Challenge Leads to Gene Discovery." *CNN.* 27 Jul. 2016. www.cnn.com/2016/07/27/health/als-ice-bucket-challenge-funds-breakthrough/.

Liszewski, Andrew. "DHL Pranked UPS into Advertising for Them." *Gizmodo.* 20 Feb. 2014. www.gizmodo.com/dhl-pranked-ups-into-advertising-for-them-1526964505.

BrandIndex. "Crowdsourcing Campaign Appears to Boost Brand Perception for Lay's." *Forbes.* 11 Oct. 2104. www.forbes.com/sites/brandindex/2014/10/11/crowdsourcing-campaign-appears-to-boost-brand-perception-for-lays/#303842b95141.

Empson, Rip. "WTF Is Waze and Why Did Google Just Pay a Billion+ for It?." *TechCrunch.* 11 Jun. 2013. techcrunch.com/2013/06/11/behind-the-maps-whats-in-a-waze-and-why-did-google-just-pay-a-billion-for-it/.

Houston, Gillie. "We Got a Sneak Peek at Lay's New Flavor Contest." *Yahoo!.* 11 Jan. 2016. www.yahoo.com/style/we-got-a-sneak-peak-1340877996630070.html.

# REFERENCES

Buhr, Sarah. "A Look Inside Transcriptic's New Biotech Testing Facility." *TechCrunch*. 25 Mar. 2015. www.techcrunch. com/2015/03/25/a-look-inside-transcriptics-new-biotech-testing-facility/.

"Emirates, Cathay, Air New Zealand Latest Airlines to 'Crowdsource New Products.'" *Airline Trends*. 26 Oct. 2010. www.airlinetrends. com/2010/10/26/airlines-crowdsourcing-new-products/.

Linkner, Josh. Interview with Mick Ebeling. 29 Jul. 2016.

"Rand McNally." *Wikipedia*. 1 Sept. 2020.

"Rand McNally Our History." 30 Sept. 2020. http://www.randmcnally.com/about/history.

"Samsung Strategy and Innovation Center." *Samsung*. 30 Sept. 2020. www.samsung.com/us/ssic/.

Giammona, Craig. "LeBron-Backed Pizza Chain Aims to Top Chipotle." *Bloomberg.com*. 14 Apr. 2015. www.bloomberg.com/news/articles/2015-04-14/lebron-backed-pizza-chain-aims-to-top-chipotle-after-sales-surge.

Lutz, Ashley. "A Chipotle-Style Pizza Chain Endorsed by LeBron James Is Taking over America." *Business Insider*. 12 Feb. 2015. www.businessinsider.com/blaze-pizza-business-story-and-strategy-2015-2.

"Biology and Robotics Come Together." *Financial Times Video*. 16 Feb. 2015. www.video.ft.com/4051712926001/Biology-and-robotics-come-together/Companies.

"Burn Therapy: An Award-Winning Regenerative Medicine Approach." *The University of Pittsburg*. 28 Oct. 2013. www.mirm.pitt.edu/news-archive/burn-therapy-an-award-winning-regenerative-medicine-approach/.

National Geographic. *The Skin Gun*. Feb. 2011. www.youtube.com/watch?v=eXO_APjKPal.

Althoefer, Kaspar. "How We Made an Octopus-Inspired Surgical Robot Using Coffee." *The Conversation*. 18 May 2015. theconversation.com/how-we-made-an-octopus-inspired-surgical-robot-using-coffee-41852.

Palermo, Elizabeth. "Flying Machines? 5 Da Vinci Designs That Were Ahead of Their Time." *Live Science*. 19 Dec. 2014. www.livescience.com/49210-leonardo-da-vinci-futuristic-inventions.html.

# CONNECTING IT ALL TOGETHER

Davidson, Kief, and Daniel Junge. *Lego Brickumentary*. Anchor Bay, 2015. Film.

"Lego Architecture." *Wikipedia*. 12 Sept. 2020.

"Lego Mindstorms." *Wikipedia*. 28 Sept. 2020.

Ringen, Jonathan. "How Lego Became the Apple of Toys." *Fast Company*. 8 Jan. 2015. www.fastcompany.com/3040223/when-it-clicks-it-clicks.

# ACKNOWLEDGMENTS

It's been such a wonderful experience bringing this book to life, but it wouldn't have been possible without the amazing support of some incredible people who helped me at every step throughout this journey. I have much appreciation and gratitude to share.

First, many thanks to Josh Linkner, who took a chance on me over twenty years ago and hired me to join his start-up, ePrize. He's been an amazing leader, mentor, and friend throughout the years, and he has continued to inspire me with his amazing creativity and never-ending desire to elevate his game. I continue to learn so much from him each and every day, and I'm extremely grateful for his guidance and generosity.

To my wife, Marilyn, who continues to inspire me to be the best version of myself, thank you for your unconditional love and never-ending support. You're what makes it all worthwhile. I admire and appreciate your relentless drive to provide the best for our family.

A special shout-out to my twins, Jared and Jada, who light up each day with so much creativity and imagination (along with some attitude!). You guys are an extraordinary blessing and have helped me to truly understand what's most important in life. I'm so proud to be your dad.

High fives to my teammates and friends at Platypus Labs: Jordan Broad, Matt Ciccone, Connor Trombley, and Lina Ksar. What an amazing experience it's been! Climb on!

A special thanks to the amazing crew at Amplify Publishing, who helped guide me through this entire process and get this book into your hands!

And finally, thank you for devoting a few hours of your time toward your own creativity and innovation capacity. I hope you found the book to be a valuable resource, and I wish you tremendous success with your innovation efforts moving forward.

# LET'S CRACK THE CODE TOGETHER

If your organization needs help embracing the mindsets and tactics in *Crack the Code*, Kaiser Yang and his team at Platypus Labs are ready to help.

## WORKSHOPS AND TRAINING EXPERIENCES

Kaiser Yang and his team conduct powerful, high-impact workshops for corporate clients, ranging from half-day sessions to multi-day experiences. These energizing, immersive sessions are designed to build muscle memory around innovative thinking while tackling real business challenges using proven methodologies and frameworks. Participants will leave with fresh approaches to drive breakthrough thinking and drive business transformation.

## INNOVATION ADVISORY SERVICES

All organizations seek growth and sustainable success. However, delivering on these goals requires a growth-enabled organization that has the right balance of innovation leadership, rituals and rewards, and systems and processes in order to create new and untapped value in the market. Kaiser Yang and his team at Platypus Labs use proven frameworks and methodologies to help organizations unlock innovation and accelerate growth. The team identifies performance gaps through a comprehensive diagnostics program, then pinpoints what is needed in order to catalyze the organization to deliver measurable results.

## SPEAKING ENGAGEMENTS

Kaiser Yang and his team bring deep executive and entrepreneurial experience to the stage, along with extensive keynote speaking experience. The Platypus Labs team has delivered thousands of inspiring and impactful speeches around the world. Their clients range from large corporations and associations to high-growth startups, universities, and governmental agencies. The team delivers an energizing performance blended with real-world experiences, leaving the audience with practical tools that they can immediately put into action in order to start driving better outcomes.

To learn more and explore a collaboration, please visit www.platypuslabs.com, or email us at innovate@platypuslabs.com.